FOREWORD

I thought it might be appropriate to explain how this book came to be born. Where did all these notes come from? Are they real? How did these letters come to be in my possession? To answer these questions, we have to travel back to 1981. As a struggling teacher working in the NYC school system with a wife and six children, l needed a second full-time job to make ends meet. As it happened, I had already been working part-time with the custodial staff at my school during the vacation periods such as Christmas, Easter and summer, so I asked the custodial engineer if he would hire me full-time on the night shift from 3pm to midnight, which he did. It meant that I would be working a long day from 8am to midnight five days a week, but "necessity is the mother of invention."

I started as a cleaner responsible for maintaining about twenty classrooms and four bathrooms. The first thing I would do in a classroom was to empty the trash can next to the teacher's desk. Out of boredom, I found myself reading the notes the students had written and discarded in the garbage. I have to tell you that these notes were fascinating. They illuminated a side of student life that I never would have known. These notes were usually emotional: angry, funny, sad, but always compelling; so much so that I began to collect them thinking of putting them together in book form one day, but I never seemed to have the time. These notes, thousands of them, have been sitting in bags in my attic for more than forty years.

With the advent of the corona virus and the accompanying lock-down, I decided to revisit these notes and finally organize them into this book. While I will not be able to share all the notes I have collected over the years, here is a representative sample. Initially, I planned to categorize these into chapters such as Teenage Romance, Parental Problems, etc. In the end, I decided instead to simply let the letters flow. I hope you enjoy reading them as much as I did.

Many thanks to my wife, Suzanne, for putting up with the thousands of notes I spread out over almost every inch of space in the house during this project. I also want to thank my daughter, Meghan, my son, Thomas and my nephew, Jack for their help and support. In addition, special kudos for William Ruyle for the photos and Amanda Tate Speedling for her artistic and tech support.

SUSAN E. WAGNER
HIGH SCHOOL
Home of the Falcons

NOTES FROM A NEW YORK CITY HIGH SCHOOL

(1981 – 1996)

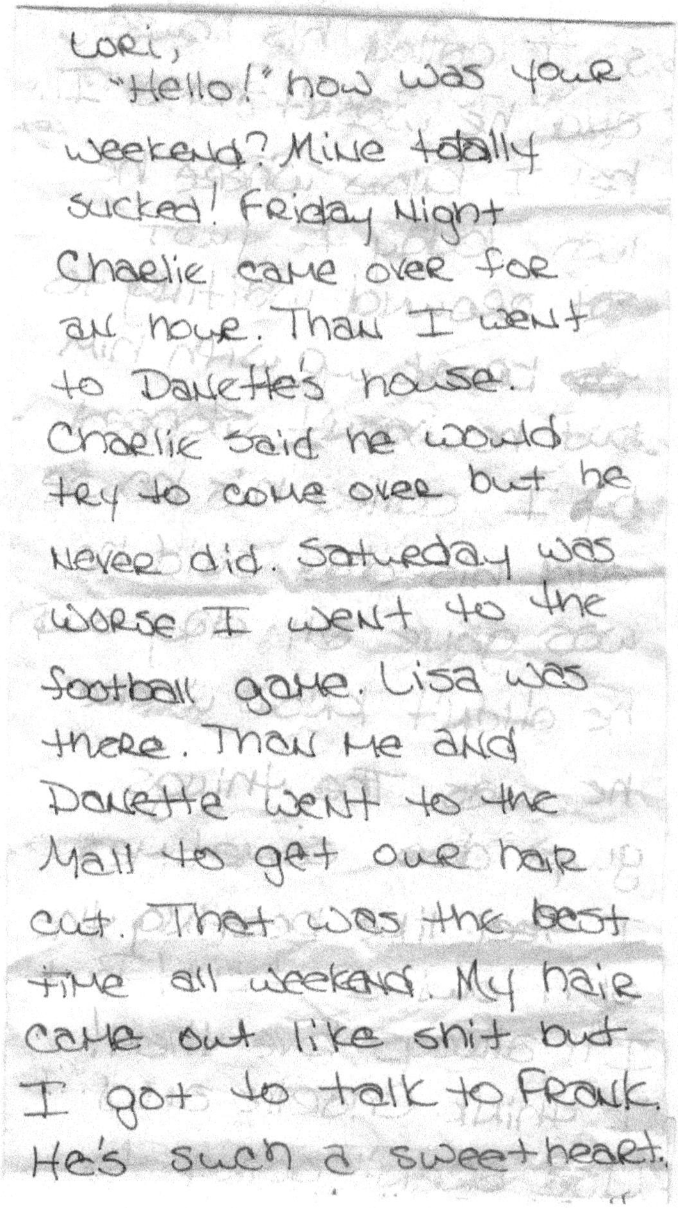

Lori,
"Hello!" how was your weekend? Mine totally sucked! Friday Night Charlie came over for an hour. Than I went to Danette's house. Charlie said he would try to come over but he never did. Saturday was worse I went to the football game. Lisa was there. Than me and Danette went to the Mall to get our hair cut. That was the best time all weekend. My hair came out like shit but I got to talk to Frank. He's such a sweetheart.

EDITED BY TOM SPEEDLING

Dear Denise 1/16/83

Hi. I'm in physics - BORING. I have two new aspects of my life to introduce to you. First of all, there's another "D". We'll call him D II. I'll tell you who he is. He's really not what you'd expect me to be interested in. He's in a few of my classes, including BASIC (I ♡ BASIC) that's computers. We get along really well. He's a really nice guy. Anyway - #2 he's in a band w/ people who don't go to this school, and he's looking for a singer. He asked me if I sang, I said "yes" and he wants to know if I'd be interested in singing w/ them. What should I do? More than anything, I love to sing. Just yesterday I was in my room singing into a mirror. My father always tells me that I sing too loud. I really love music. You know that. I do everything while listening to music. Name *anything* and I bet you I listen to music in order to do it. Name any song on the radio, and I know the words. Anyway - back to issue #1. We were having a panic in BASIC today, we were talking about SING. (Hint: he was in Junior Sing this year) I had a really nice time, and the "real me" really showed through. Later on, I saw him in the hall and a he put his hand on my cheek & said hello. Just in a matter of seconds, as we were walking past each other. I was thinking about him before the vacation, but decided I'd give it better thought when we got back. Well, now we're back, and I'm giving it some much better thought. Here are the words to "only you"

when was the last time I said,
I loved ________

Denise I'll put it on separate paper OK? And on the back is the Led Zepplin song

Let me know

Love
Ro

Dear Helen,

Hi, what's up? So he cancelled Friday, that's beat. I really was looking forward to hearing what happened. Oh well, I was supposed to call Vinny last night but I fell asleep when I was watching T.V. I really like him, but he expects alot from me, I guess. It'll be one month the 22nd that I'm seeing him, wow! I can't believe it. I might see him tonight - That would be something if he asked me to give him a BJ and I did. Yuck

LP
Charlene

Charlene,

If I were you when I would see him I wouldn't give him a B.J. I feel as though you would get hurt. I don't want to see you get hurt. It really sounds as if he is only asking for one thing. I fear you getting into something that would hurt you emotionally. With my situation I am going to see him even if it is after the holidays. But I will see him. For it's time. Helen.

Dear Helen,

Hi, what's up? So he cancelled Friday, that's beat. I really was looking forward to hearing what happened. Oh well, I was supposed to call Vinny last night but I fell asleep when I was watching T.V. I really like him, but he expects alot from me, I guess. It'll be one month the 22nd that I'm seeing him, wow! I can't believe it. I might see him tonight - That would be something if he asked me to give him a BJ and I did. Yuck

UP Charlene

Charlene,

If I were you when I would see him I wouldn't give him a B.J. I feel as though you would get hurt. I don't want to see you get hurt. It really sounds as if he is only asking for one thing. I fear you getting into something that would hurt you emotionally. With my situation I am going to see him even if it is after the holidays. But I will see him. For it is time. Helen.

Helen,

You are right - I probably wouldn't do that only cause to me, it wouldn't be right - I would feel hurt -
But I'm so confused!
I don't know what to expect - I guess nowaday there aren't too many girls that are "pure" if you know what I mean - I want to remain that way, but as time goes on, it gets tougher and tougher.
What do you think? - the first time should be "special" agree?

[illegible]

My opinion is that the first time is special because I would give my *whole* self to him. This is not felt by many girls.
But I stick to my guns enough to get by. It is tough because it is something so natural when

1/13/83

Dear Henry,

I am writing this cause I don't know the next time I'll see you. I'm almost positive my father knows something of me & you. ~~Not~~ I already made up my mind to cool it with me & you. Not only cause you can get hurt, but for my own ~~personal~~ selfish reasons.

Henry, I made a decision today to go upstate. I know if I continue to live where I'm living I'll end up self-destroying me. & I don't want my father have the satisfaction of saying how "sick ~~she~~ I was".

Henry please understand, I can't take the way I feel much longer. I can't take the torment & anguish my father creates within me. I ~~can't~~ can't be a phony any longer & pretend how happy I am (although I am very happy with you there.) I can't play it off how straight I am. I'm so tired of sneaking around (not just with

you.) other things, cause my
father won't understand. I
don't let people know how really
fucked-up I am on the inside,
I am scared everyone is gonna
look down at me & say how sick
I am (like my father). I am so
scare of living & all only alone &
nobody giving a fuck, or if they do,
abusing & tormenting me to show they
love me. I don't want
to feel love out of abusement.
Henry I am very sorry but if
you care about me, please try
& understand me. This is a
very hard decision for me to make,
but I have to make it. I'll
always have feelings for you, & think of me & you
together, but right now it's not
the time. Maybe someday we'll meet up
again, I'm sorry Henry! Please
try & understand.

Love You Always
Paula

HIGH JESSICA?! 10/10

SO, WHAT'S UP? I'M IN MY GLOBAL HISTORY CLASS NOW. I HAVE A TOTALLY MAGNIFICENT PLAN TO DO TO [redacted] THE GREASY HAIRED BITCH (I AM NOT MENTIONING HER NAME, IN CASE SOMEBODY SEES THIS LETTER). NO ONE CAN KNOW ABOUT THIS. I'll TELL YOU LATER. IT'S SO FUCKIN' DEVIOUS! CLAUDIA ACTUALLY THOUGHT UP THE IDEA, BUT SHE WANT TO DO IT TO THAT GIRL MICHELLE [redacted]. ANYWAY, WHAT'S NEW? I AM SO BORED. I DON'T KNOW WHAT TO WRITE ANYMORE. HO HUM. I WANT TO GO TO SLEEP. WELL, SO HOW'S PHIL? MAN, I AM SO BORED. I GUESS I AM GOING TO GO NOW! BYE!

Keri

Keri ♡ loves ♡ Mark 9♡1♡84	♡ Jessica ♡ loves ♡ Phil 7♡15♡84	♡ Claudia ♡ loves ♡ Kenny	♡ Kami ♡ loves ♡ Pat

BLACK SABBATH

OZZY

RATT

ARMORED SAINT

IRON MAIDEN

HEAVY

METALLICA

RAVEN

SCORPS

ANVIL

FUCKIN'

Saxon

Mercyful Fate

METAL

RIOT

MÖTLEY CRÜE

Queensryche

MSG

DIO

Accept

MANOWAR

ANGELWITCH

Judas Priest

Helix

EXCITER

Lori 4
-Loves- ev
Dave er
Alot.
Now &
4 Always!

12-15-83

Lori,

"Hello" how are you?
Dave is in. I saw him
this morning.

Lastnight Charlie didn't
come over. I am so mad!
I felt like crying. It gets
me upset because it
seems like he doesn't
even care. I'm not even
going to call him anymore.
If he wants to talk to
me he can ask Danette
or Lowie for my number
or he could just come
over but forget it
I'm not even gonna
go to him first. If
he wants me he can
come and get me but
until then I'm not
even going to think
about him.

Lastnight Chris
brought my stuff

over and we got stoned! I fucking had [illegible] asma I almost died! I'm serious! I couldn't breath. I was looking for the medicine and I couldn't find it. I was going crazy. I started praying. I was so scared that I was going to die. My windpipe started to close and my face looked kinda blue. Lori, I'm serious I thought I was dying. Do you know what its like to walk around stoned and then you get asma. Its pain!

Well I got to go. See you in home-room.

Lori 4 ev er loves Dave Not, Now & Always!

Love ya!,
Your Cousin
Kelly

SUSAN E. WAGNER
HIGH SCHOOL

How am I supposed to smoke my cigarette? Theres no filter? You should try Strawberry rolling papers they're delicious.

Do you still want the acid .. when are you going to take it and with who

I don't know

me, myself & I

yes

I'll give you the $5 or $4 (which one) after class.

Theres only one other person I know who takes acid & I only hang out with her usually in school.

Give me $5 to be safe and if its only $4 I'll give you your $1 back.

O.K. What else can you get besides acid, mesc & coke? Is the coke good? Can you get uppers, downers, etc.?

The coke I heard is very good. The uppers and downers I'll have to see about.

This guy sounds like a drug machine. Who do you get it from? Shmoo? Does he also ~~can~~ sell pot?

shmoo only sells mesc. I'm going to start selling this week. This guy who sells all the other drugs is in my homeroom. He knows alot of People. Acid is Pretty cool but you can't keep taking it. Only once in a while. It makes you laugh alot more.

My friend Helen told me that if you take acid 5 times in your life that you are considered legally insane. Did you ever take acid? Find out what other stuff he can get.

Write back soon!

Date ~ 4*25*85
time ~ 8*55
why ~ because its only right*

what's up sharon! nothing this way except that this damn teacher gets on my nerves* that's why I'm writing letters in his class* so hows your love life + david if thats his name* my love life is growing stronger by the day* see if me + kenny didnt have that understanding we wouldnt be together right now* But we do And we are together* see I know bitches are waiting to see if we breakup soon* but no cause where not gonna because we love each other that much * See Kenny said that he wants to marry me after I graduate * And of course I am because thats my sweet heart * Kenny's suppose to be putting down on my name earrings tomorrow * so hell probably get them out next week *

gotta go! *
sorry ending
so
short

8 Baby * Bree
30 ♡loves♡
84 K * Smack

#I!

Lets see what my problems are today

① I failed my Calc test this morn.

thats about it right now!

I am taking my Rhodes test in 2 weeks – watch out!

I can't wait. My social life has hit rock bottom. I am absolutely convinced that Skip is either homosexual or celebid. I mean the boy has no interest in the opposite sex. Shy – O.K. – but this is crazy. You know how when guys get really shitfaced & a girl is like hanging on them – they like go for it? Well, this really tacky girl has been hanging all over Skip & he has been real shitfaced & he hasn't even tried to go for her. I have seen all of his friends (all – meaning 50) go with girls in the past year but not Skip. I have just given up & I'm so hurt by it. What are you doing Xmas? Lets plan at leste one special thing O.K.?

W/

b E—

P.S. What should I do about my infatuation w/ a priest—

CBK

way to go - Wallace!

Well, If you're having problems w/ Skip, you should ask Beth [redacted] the saint for help. You should have heard her in leadership today talking as if she was a saint - Gimme a break! I think we had both better meet new guys - soon! I'm starting not even to care who - just as long as they are not half bad - I can't believe [redacted] I am saying this! You know what I mean - we just have to find someone(s)! Where? I mean if Nowie has someone - [redacted] we are in deep trouble - Ha-Ha!

I am so tired (and hungry - of course!). What do you want to do Christmas - are you going to Sharon's? What are you doing this weekend. I think you need a vacation from Skip - he is just not worth all of the effort (I know he's cute & all but if he's really not interested - not in anyone - then just drop it). O.K. - I know you can't do it but try!

11/3

M

He's definitely worth it but I'm stating to think he's a lost cause. I would bear my soul to him - O-a he's so worth it. He got a haircut by the way

he's into eyeliner big time now! I swear I love him.

I think that I should make a major play for him. If it backfires - well, that's life. We need guy though - I could even see myself w/ a Jewish guy from L.I. at this point. I am spending Xmas eve at Sharon's (I think). Lets do something! This weekend is that party for that record for Ethopia at Hard Rock Cafe. I hope Nina comes in -

By the way I put pictures in my wallet & I want one of you so lets make copies of the Halloween one or something. Are you ever going to see Mr. [redacted] again maybe over Xmas. What was Ms. [redacted] saying during leadership?

She was telling the class how she wasn't ever prejudice - gimme a break - what a crock! I will probably see Adam over vacation

because Felicia & Glen & Abany
people will be together & he & him will be there. But I am not going to think about it because I'm sure nothing will happen. Does

it

ever?

We are cursed

E. WAGNER
SCHOOL
of the Falcons

666

Coopius,

WHAT IS THY PROBLEM? WHERE HAST THIS PROBLEM COMETH FROM? PERHAPS FROM YOUR CLEOPATRA?

ERNIUS CEASAR

Yes. Very much So. Joanne said SHE WANTED TO Be "Good friends". But When thy Beauty saideth this, I knoweth she really didn't mean this did I realize. Why thou mightith ask? To me, She hast feelings of fear inside of her anatomy. Me & Her tooketh a long walk ye day before yesterday. And toldeth me did she that 1) She Never went out with a guy before. and 2) SHE NEVER Kissed a guy Before. SHOCKED WAS I. so pretty is SHE, I thoughteth one guy or another mightith hast "tested THOSE WATERS". knoweth SHE LIKES me I do. But Scared is SHE. Liketh HER I really Do. AND SHE Liketh me. Hard is it going to be to try & Changeth her mind.

WOULDST THOU LIKEST ME TO CONVERSE with ye female of LOVLINESS? THOU DOST INDEED KNOWEST THAT INDEED I AM ONEITH OF THE SHAPEST SPEAKERITHS WHEN COMITH IT DOEDS TO MATCHING-ITH PEOPLE.

WOULDST THOU? Appreciateth that I would. But DON'T Bring up what we discussed in THIS LETTER. PLEASE Telleth me THAT SHE SHOULD Give me a CHANCE. AND Telleth WHAT I AM LikesT. (IN your opinion.) Telleth I really Like Her alot.

This I shall doith! When ~~tho~~ through I am, loveth ye shall she! And happily ever after shall ye liveth!!

Hopefully. THOU art Truly A FRIEND. OF FRIENDS. HOPEST THIS TALK WILL WORK WE MUST. Tell HER you know me well & SAW ME DEPRESSED IN Gym.

HO-ke-DO-Ke Coopius!

Oct. 4, 1984

Dear Emily,

Hello dear!

~~I'm~~ I've just finished an English Essay test. I never said absolutely nothing in 2 pages before. Total bullshit. Not one clue to what the book was about, would be about or could be about. I did 1 3/4 pages. Wrote big, used big words, and said the same things about 3 times each just worded different.

To top it all off, it was written beautifully.

My hands are shaking, I was racking my brain like never before. Shit I hope I pass. He'd probably give me a 100 too! ha!

God, I hope so. Or close to it.

- I finished my role of film. Yay! Can you come in with me to roll it?
- I missed you at lunch, you better be in, you bitch.
- Mary had some very small talk with me today. HA!

I cant even think. I had to write something on that paper. And I did. Shit! Did I bullshit.

Speaking of ↑ - Guess who spoke to me in the hallway. Yes, your friend, not mine, Pete. He goes, "Oh yeah, I love Rock-N-Roll"

What are we, fucking nuts or wha

people are really getting to me.
I feel like taking up skydiving.
or hot-air ballooning, or something
like that where I can go up into
the air away from the fucking assholes,
away from hassles and bullshit,
away from problems,
where I can think to myself
in millions of miles of space
all to myself and breath
every fucking toxic gas up there
that I can.

♡ STACEY.

OCT 5, 1984
Herro Dare you woodpecker!
Any way, times have changed and things
are rough - you know they're not like they
used to be,
And when the tough get going, they
usually forget to close the door.
Well, that's life, no use crying over
spilt milk, unless its all over
one of your teachers.
Right?

♡. STACEY

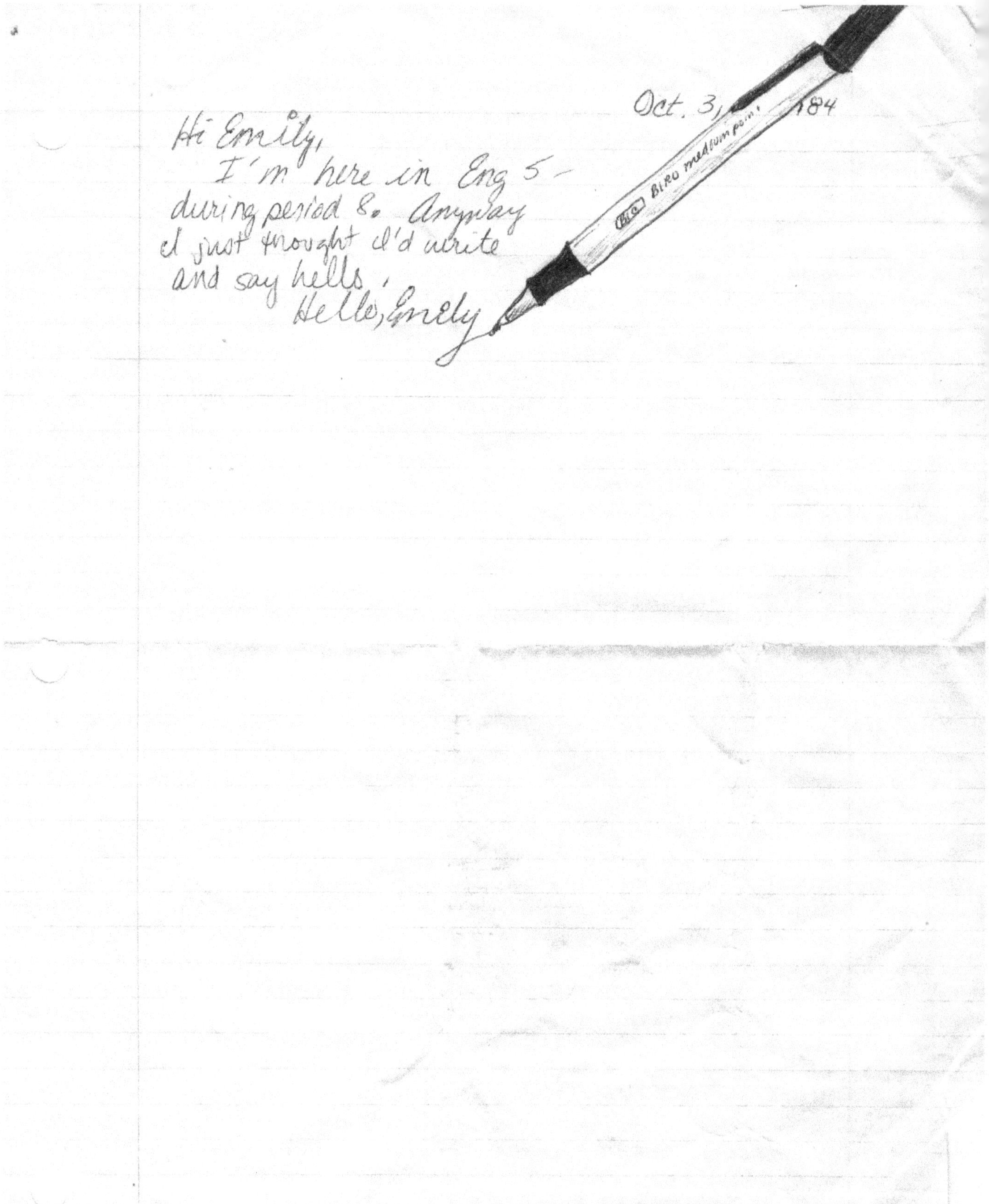
Oct. 3, '84
Hi Emily,
I'm here in Eng 5 -
during period 8. Anyway
I just thought I'd write
and say hello.
Hello, Emily
BIC Biro medium point

♡ STACEY

Dear Emily,

We have to find out if he's going out w/ anyone! Ask him for me

Jackie

PS. I have ~~$~~3 very importent things to talk to you about!

Emily,

I have 3 problems. Ya see I have to know what religion Denis is inorder for me to go out w/ him. my father will not let me go out w/ him unless he's jewish. So if he's not I can't. How can I find out if he's jewish, Catholic Italian etc. How can I find out if he likes me? My last problem is 9 girls want to kick my ass in why I don't know. I never said two words to them. oh well if they'll kick my ass they'll kick my ass. ~~they~~ if they really were anxious they wouldhve done it already. right! glad we agree. speak to ya Later.

Jackie

but now I don't ~~I~~ know ~~if he's~~ he's religion

Don't forget to ask Denis
1) if he's going out w/ anyone
2) if he likes me - nah tell him I like him

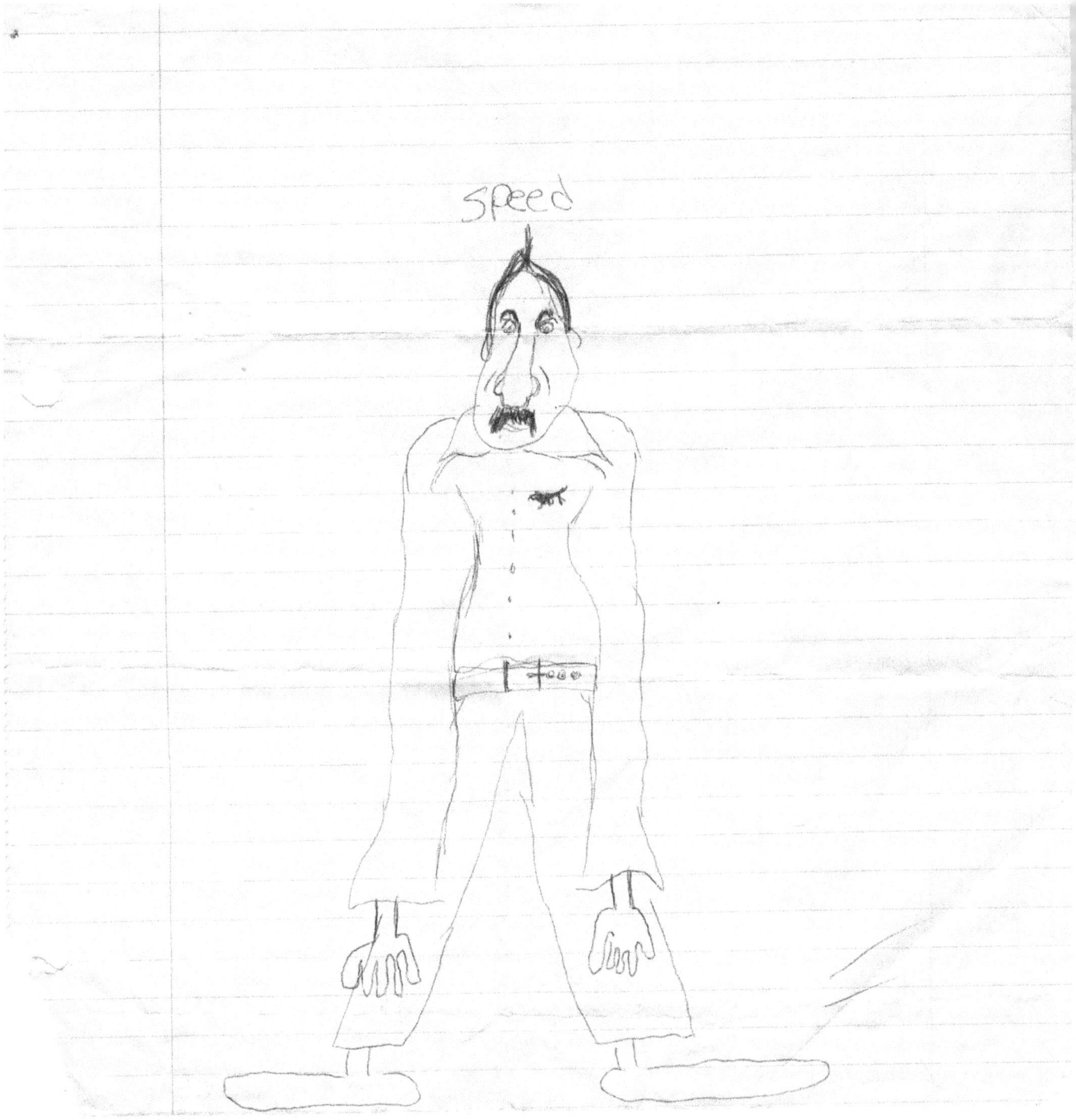
speed

1) Germany
2) Russia
3) Serbian
4) 14 points
5 Russia
6 a
7 C
8 D
9 e
10 H
11 B
12 D
13 B
14 C
15 C
16 C
17 D
18 D
19 D
20 C
21 D
22 B
23 a
24 C
25 B
26 T
27 1914
28 T

CURB, TAT - ADJ EXCEEDING W B CONFORMITY
FACTITIOUS - ADJ DEVELOPED BY [illegible]
FEIGN V A FALSE APPEARANCE
FLAGRANT - ADJ SCANDALOUS
GREGARIOUS - ADJ LIVING IN HERDS
HARANGUE - N LONG POMPOUS SPEAC
HYPOCRISY N PRETENDING TO BE WHAT ONES NOT
IDIOSYNCRASY - N A personal peculiarity
IMBIBE - V DRINK
IMPUNITY - N FREEDOM FROM PUNISHMENT
INCEPTION - N COMMENCEMENT
INCREDULITY - N LACK OF BELIEF
INSIDIOUS - ADJ TRECHEROUS
INFALLIBLE - ADJ FREE FROM ERROR
LATENT - ADJ PRESENT BUT NOT ACTIVE
LEVY - V ORDER TO BE PAID
LIBIDINOUS - ADJ LUSTFUL, LEWD
[illegible] - ADJ [illegible] TO COME TO OTHERS
[illegible] - N SHORT RULE OF CONDUCT, PROVERB
MERITORIOUS - ADJ DESERVING AWARD OR PRAISE
MORBID - ADJ GLOOMY & ILL-HUMORED
MUNIFICENT - ADJ EXTREMELY GENEROUS
OBDURATE - ADJ STUBBORN
OBSEQUIOUS - ADJ [illegible] OF OBEDIENT FROM
[illegible] OF SH. [illegible] FROM [illegible]

G. △ABC
P. m∠A + m∠B + m∠C = 180
S R

1) Let $\overline{DE}$ be the line through B ∥ to AC — Thru a pt. not on a line there exists one and only 1 line ∥ to given
2) m∠DBE = 180 — st. ∠ measures 180
3) m∠1 + m∠2 + m∠3 = 180 — whole equal is sum of parts
4) ∠A ≅ ∠1, ∠C ≅ ∠2; m∠A = m∠1, m∠C = m∠2 — 2 ∥ lines cut by trans. alt. int. ∠'s are ≅
5) m∠A + m∠B + m∠C = 180 — Substitution Pos.

Sum of m of △ = 180

I care, but I don't care

I care about you, and many things you do. but I don't care about the environments. If you want to go, go If you want to stay, you may. I do care if you go. but, I don't care cause if you really want to go you will. I care if Elaine tries to get you back, But I don't care about her silly act's, cause if you want to you can throw her off the ~~the~~ wrong track. what ever you say, or do I'll always care about you. So. you may act as you please, I hope my attitude is not causing you grief. ~~Sorry~~ it it's, But now I'm feeling pressure I can't explain. since you told me ~~~~ the girl who's coming over is Elaine. no matter what she says or do. She can't get no further than you want her to. and I hope you understand I care, but I don't care. I'm tired of pain I feel I've had my share!

~~I'm confused, can't you tell?!~~

I'm confused Can't you tell?!

I'm confused, can't you tell?! If it was up
to me to let Elaine come. "I'd say "no way in hell."
But, she's coming to see you Jerome., I can't
throw her out of your home.
So I'll be upset for a while, but I won't
feel down. Cause, when she comes to greet you
I won't be around!" But I'll return, ~~as~~ inching quietly as an inchworm,
as
you can ~~continue doing~~ do anything ~~that~~ you or
please. Cause I can't become more upset, ~~can't~~ I
can't hold any more grief. So never mind the
I don't know what to do,
way ~~I act toward you~~, I really shouldn't be
upset with you., but you see I'm confused.
I shouldn't be mad., I should forget
and say "I've already been through Hell," but I
I'm confused
Can't Cause I'm confused, can't you tell?!
After she's came and gone I won't
I shouldn't
be confused, because it ~~what~~ wasn't be no use.
I ~~would~~ will escape from all my misery and hell
and will be feeling ~~no other way but~~ well. that only after she
leaves you see., then I'll be the sweet Jeanine
right now
I used to be but, it's no used I'm ~~now~~ confused!

SCHOOL'S A SPLITTING
HEADACHE!

But dont the Pill protect you 24 hours and only if a women or young girl ovulates is only when she can become pregnant.

The pill protects you 24 hours before you have whoopie but you didn't take it thursday or friday so you just might be.

I missed thursday and then when friday night at 11:00 I took thursday + friday do you think it would be in time to stop ?

you took two pills on friday. youre an asshole that's not going to protect you for what you did all Ready.

OH Shit

OH Shit

J.R. time

Dear Mike

I don't know if I should write you a letter or tell you in person, but you're wrong I didn't mean to avoid you this morning, but I was in a very down and out type of mood. The only reason I wanted Wendy to sit next to me this morning was because she looked like she was gonna fall apart any minute. I meant what I said too. But I need a little time to adjust to it, know what I mean?! Cause, when you told me yesterday it blew my mind, I had no idea. I can't come out this afternoon, but I'll be out tonight, but by that time you'll be trippin, right?!

I'll call you,

Love
Noreen

But dont the Pill protect you 24 hours and only if a women or young girl ovulates is only when she can become pregnant.

The pill protects you 24 hours before you have whoopie but you didn't take it thursday or Friday so you just might be.

I missed thursday and then when friday night at 11:00 I took thursday + friday do you think it would be in time to stop ?

you took two pills on Friday, your an asshole that's not going to protect you for what you did all Ready.

OH Shit

OH Shit

J.R. time

37

Ag
SCIENCE
Social

Kecia,

I think when I talk to him on the phone tonight that he is going to ask me something serious. What? I don't know. But I have this feeling that he's going to ask me something about sex. If you know what I mean. But you know what my answer is. When I was just talking to Nicause she was telling me that he has something important to say. I know he would tell her because they are good friends and they have lunch together. So what are

you going to do
you have him this
if go through with it
if you Dont think bout
whats in your heart
Dont give in to presure
What you have is your sexy pride
and joy Keep it while you can.
you really should think about
this befor you give him a answer.
are you anxious to have Sex with him
Do you really want him badly

Well I do want him but not enough to sleep with him yet.

Kim,

I know everything that you are saying and don't try to deny it. Everybody can't stand you with your little lies and friendly kisses. Its sickening! You use people to get what you want! Don't let me catch you alone walking in the halls if you still want your teeth!

Watch out

I'm after your big lying mouth!

love always

<<the gang>>

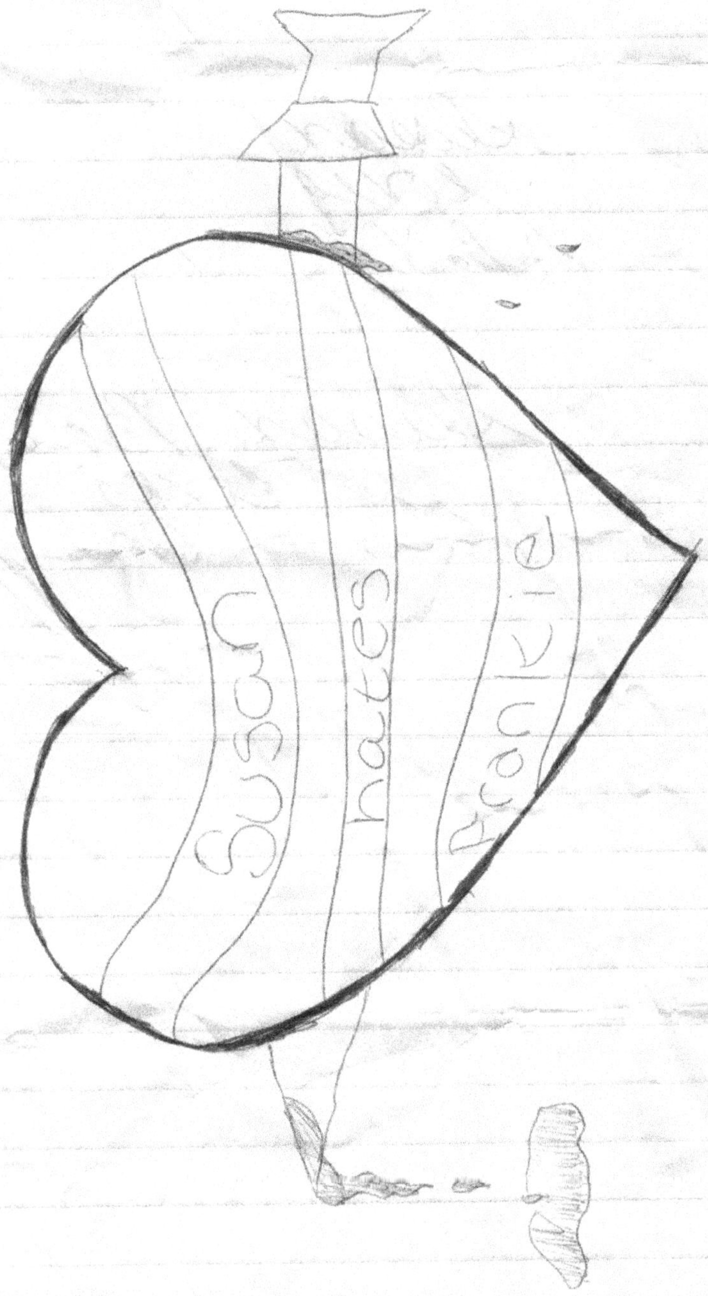
Susan
hates
Frankie

Jodi,
Don't worry about Anthony. If you lose 20 lbs. no one will see you! Your thin now. Remember what you said about your sister?! She's probably only 5 to 7 lbs. lighter than you at the most. You told me she looks so bony in her bathing suits + summer clothes. I don't know where you got such an idea to begin with.

I'm on a diet now. I gain approximately 18 lbs. in the last year and a half (cause I was in the hospital over 3 months in the last two summers). I lost 6 lbs. already - I have another 20 to go before May.

I don't have any passes because I haven't worked in an Office downstairs since Jan. I'll ask around for you today.

Have a good time tomorrow - oh, who's party? I hope the weather's nice.

WB Lisa

My sister looks bony because of her body shape - mine isn't like hers.
I am so fat + out of shape. fat is unhealthy + I think it looks disgusting! I'm going to lift weights + I don't want muscles, just very tight + strong
thanks for asking for the passes. it's a big party - I don't know exactly who's. mike shaunbuck invited everybody. I hope tomorrow is just like today

Jodi

this is so easy
ps you look good today!

6-1-83

Dear Darren,

I love You

These things are the things I need from you and the things that I hope I can return to you! I hope they can help us realize what we really mean to each other.

I want you to know you are my life, my morning my night my soul my flesh my heart. With out you I would not exist and I wouldn't want to. I love You

Right now I'm confused and scared about a lot of things but you help me through this and I know whatever we do our love will survive and it will pull me through and one day we will be happy forever with out no more tears or depressions or bad moods. I promise you this.

I love you.

Right now I just want to squeeze you and kiss you so much. I really mean it when I say

I love you. As the months go on ~~that~~ 3 letter statement gets so much more feeling in it and I hope ~~that~~ some understanding will come with ~~[illegible]~~ it too.

I love you

I love you

All my LOVE
Always
Lea

To
Darren ~~[illegible]~~
my only love
[illegible]

It Started Like This.

Some Kid on the Stallions, whent up to My (Kamakazie) Quarter Back and Kicked him in The Balls. His Cup Broke And He got hurt Reall Bad. My Freind Shane And I Picked Him up (The Q.B.) And Put him On his CAR. By This Time EVERyBody WAS on EVERyBody! Me And Stu went Into The fight And Mixed it up A Little, And The Kid That Shane And me helped, went over into his Glove Compartment And Picked up A →

45. Caliber pistol And
Pointed it At someones head.
A Stallion kicked it out
of his hand, And Pointed it
At me Qaurterback And
The kid heard
The cop sirens, And
Threw The Gun in The Bushes.
By This time, Me + Stv
were Out of There Before
The cops came.

Where did this take place?
Did anyone get caught by the
cops? How many people are after
~~use~~ you's? Are you going to
carry a knife? w/B.

At The Elks Club Feild on Arthur Kill And
The West Shore Expressway. Some of my freinds
were caught by cops, And so were some
Theirs. About 2 Gangs (Approxamatley 50
Fuckin-A Yeah I'm carrying A knife
are you scaird? Fuckin-A Yeah!

Vered,

I dont know why, but I wish I were going on the Junior trip. Coral's room combined has 12 oz of pot - Shh! Sandy Scarantino brought Vodka, Peach Schnapps, beer, wine coolers & bourbon Her alone - plus the others in her room. She said Elena Anasumo was checking bags - an 18 year old! Hah! She said Elena said to her "I know you brought alot of shit, so just go + have fun!" Can you believe it. They only open your bag, but don't go through it - I could've had a hell of a good time on this trip! I wouldn't smoke pot, but I'd drink a little I wouldn't get drunk, but you already know that. Why didn't I go? I'm such an asshole. My parents once said that when a good opportunity arrises, you should jump at the chance & go for it. Why did my mother tell me to choose either Quebec or the Junior Trip? I don't even care about the money anymore! I would pay for it myself if I had to - I know it not worth the money, but for once I want to fit in & party with the rest of them. I'm definetely going on the Senior trip - I don't care if its $1000 dollars. Are you going? I don't have to stay in your room because Sam probably will. But we have plenty of time to worry about that. I don't think I would want to stay in your room anyway because that would be the BOREDOM Room. W/B/Please! Lam

10-30-84

You,

What's wrong? How come you dont talk to me anymore If I did something to make you mad, then I'm sorry. You probably wont believe this, but I do still like you.

PLEASE W/B

Love Always

♡ Carol ♡

ANSWER ONE QUESTION WHOS THAT guy you were with. Forget it I DON'T WANT to KNOW! HAVE FUN IN Life

That guy is someone that I used to go with. The other day when you said that I was fucked up (I heard you) in the courtyard, I decided that you weren't interested anymore. It's true isn't it? You didn't talk to me for about a week so obviously you didn't want to have anything to do with me and I got the hint. Dont play baby games with me anymore =

I've had enough of the bullshit. If you're gonna say you like me one day and then not talk to me for a week then forget everything. It's definately not worth it and you know it.

Love,
Carol

W/B

up your so Full of Shit

~~[illegible]~~ LATTER AND you KNOW it.

NO

Ha,
Go find yourself a girlfriend who's gonna take your shit.

GOOD LUCK

But I'll tell you one thing:
things could have been good
REAL GOOD!

Dear John
Hiya, What's up? Not much here. You look pissed off today, whats wrong? You should come by my house tomorrow night with some weed. My parents aren't gonna be home so we could have that long talk. Well if you want too just tell me. I'm probably gonna call you today or tomorrow so you better be home! Shit I'm so dizzy today. I lost 5 lbs aren't you proud of me? Your hair looks good or in my words CUTE! What made you get it cut? Wow like I have totally no idea what the hell is going on in this moron class. I think I belong in Fundelmental Math. Defitnaly not Algebra even if I am back in Algebra A. My father took a total shit fit when I hang Ozzy + Randy on my wall. He got so hyper. He told me if I didn't take them down he would break my head

So I thought it might be a good place too listen too him. Even if he is an asshole. Well I better go before I get totally depressed trying to figure this shit out. W/b/s

Love ya lots
Always
=n=
Forever
Jess

Ozzy!! Rules

Disco Rock
s s
x l
e
s

Randy Rhoads lives on

debbie was telling
me she got drunk
and all this stuff
I meet ~~john~~ john
while i was their
he lives around the
block from my
grandmothers
house and we
were fooling
around and playing
~~man~~ MAN hunt - we always
do that
Yesterday I slept till
11:30 then watched
Mommie Dearest. I told

4.50
Adm. 4.24
Tax .26
AMBOY CINEMAS
103234

4.50
Adm. 4.24
Tax .26
AMBOY CINEMAS
103235

4.50
Adm. 4.24
Tax .26
AMBOY CINEMAS
103234

4.50
Adm. 4.24
Tax .26
AMBOY CINEMAS
103235

My Mother I was going
to Buy her close
wire hangers for
Christmas Because
Joan Crafurd beat her
daughter with a
wired hanger
Boe

She was a crazy
women I hated
when she strapped
her son in his
bed and when she
Killed chris with
the iron hanger
Lisa

PRINCIPAL'S OFFICE
SUSAN E. WAGNER HIGH SCHOOL

Katrina
LVS
Eddie always

Vicky 5/5/83
LVS
Steven

Dear Katrina,

hi, what's up? hows life? Is Eddie coming down Friday? you want to go to see "Breatheless" instead of going to the ~~mo~~ beach!! I want to. that movie looks good!! Are you going to the flea market Saturday!? You know Carries striped pants that she wore yesterday, I want to get a pair- ya like 'em? I hope I get my hair cut today. I have to see if my mother will drive me down!! well I'm gonna go W/B/S. Love, "me"'

Beth,

Whatsa matter Bethamania. I mean... whaaat!! (put your hand in your hair) ya know. (put your hand in your hair again). Did you speak to Sherri? Who was she talking about lastnite? You don't have to tell me if you don't want. Things are moving slowly but surely. I mean ya know... 1 week ago nothing was moving

A list of things that are getting together and not getting together

Together	Not Together
STAGE CREW	BAND
DANCERS	CHORUS
Costumes	

ART

w/B

Joe

PASS
WITH
HARD
WORK
TURN IT
OFF
U-TURN
U GET
original
individual
MEET THE PERSON
RESPONSIBLE FOR YOUR
GRADES
SUCCESS
ACTIONS

Beth,

Whatsa matter Bethamania. I mean ... whaaat !!. (put your hand in your hair) ya know. (put your hand in your hair again). Did you speak to Sherri? Who was she talking about lastnite? You don't have to tell me if you don't want. Things are moving slowly but surely. I mean ya know .. 1 week ago nothing was moving

A list of things that are getting together and not getting together

Together	Not Together
STAGE CREW	BAND
DANCERS	CHORUS
Costumes	

ART

W/B

Joe

Joe, I ♡ ya!
Thank for everything

Joe,
I'm just exhausted I have a lot on my mind about sing & my life. Sing is great but everything else is wrong. My marks, my parents, my friends are dropping, getting annoyed, being Snotty!!
Oh well. Sherry was talking about Hayley about winning & I think Amy about dancing! I don't know. She's sick today. I hope she's coming tonite. Anyway

I'll talk to U tonite How are U doing? Is everything normal by U?
W/B
Love,
Beth

Beth, I'm sorry about your parents and everything, but you can always count on me to try to put a smile on your face. We might have only 2 or 3 months of friendship under our belt but hopefully we can carry our friendship out after sing. Don't worry about sing - if you have a problem w/ anyone (in sing) just come to me and talk about it. I'll say nothing (that is until I write my book about you!)
Love always
Joe

Dear Sam,

Is this boring or what? Don't forget about Sing. Don't tell anyone ~~yo~~ who was absent last night. You know about Happy New Year. Did [redacted] Steph bring her costume and skirt? Did I tell you what Terri did to me? Well we work for Mrs. K[redacted] (Karen and I) 4th period and Terri and Liz work 6th period. Well she (Terri) got Karen and me in trouble, [redacted] I thought friends didnt do that. I talked to her at the Sing meeting, I said, "Why did you get Karen..." and she stopped me and said "Fuck Karen". then I said "Why did you get Karen and me in trouble?" She said, "Thats tough shit." And I left it like that. Later she asked me "Do you have a dime?" really sweet. I said "I don't have one and if I did I wouldn't give you ~~it~~ it if I did." she said "Thats how you feel about it." [redacted] I said "Yes shithead"

Now just the other day (dress rehersal) she said in her sweet way "I have to talk to you." I said, "Sam and I made up but I don't think we can." When you got us in trouble thats when YOU gave our friendship up!"

What you you think?

Sam

or Bud

(Got ya but only kidding)

I am goines to lunch next.

Why? are we having a test? Knots LANDING tonight?

No we are not having a test I just don't want to go to Spanish.
Gill did you see Dynasty last night
Sammy Jo got tied up by Adam and he took the baby home to Steven.
That black lady tell Blake that they shared the same father. I feel sorry for Alexis, "I want to see my baby".
Next week Steven said he know who kill Mark Jennings.

I think who killed mark is that congressman + steven is gonna testify as a mystery person.
That was nice of adam to do that. it was the lease he could do!

The congressman is too oveious
I think somebody else did it.
I saw knots landing for tonight and Abby is telling Gary that married must be based on trust. Gary ask
el if she is crazy.

He did on snap! Don't go to lunch comeon, you know now mr. monkey man is a cuts + you failed cotout tomarrow!!

I won't cut out then.
I hope Val mother tell Val that Guy is her son.
On Dynesty Alexis trial start next week. they are going to find her Guilt
That Guy that was so. post to Give Blake the loan said no because Alexis change his mind. and Blake is Going to get back at her at the trial.

Alexis fucked that guy you mean But wait to Blake gets her he said

You're burnt. Don't laugh.
If I give you $3 can you
get me one? What kind
did you take?
what do you mean I'm burnt.
You are a burn out. answer
the above 2 questions
what do you mean I'm a
burnoot. what makes you think
that
I don't know. Just that you're
stoned. Now answer the above
2 questions.

I told the kid to try to
get 4 to bring in Tuesday.
There very hard to get now.
I smoked some pot last period.
It wasn't from school. It
was from willowbrook. willow
Puts something in there pot
Today is tuesday, Can I give
you $3 anyhow just in case?
He might have them tomorrow,
Why do you want them so
bad. Why don't you buy some
pot.
I like them that why. I'll give you $3
just incase

Okay, my friend is leading
me $3. If he can't lend
me some money could I
borrow $3. You know I pay
you back

I only have $3. I need a hit.
Please try to get it for me
I mean by tomorrow or
Thursday.

Can you try to get it for
me today

I'll try. Could you lend
me $3.

I only have $3 though for
1 hit. I need to have one. I haven't
had one in over 1 week

The kid near the door with
the light blonde hair looks
as if he's a fang and he
keeps making faces like
a monkey!

He looks like a monkey. See
if you get the money from
your friend. I'll see if I have
$3 tomorrow or Thursday. I'll give
you $3 today to see if you can
get me a hit.

mondo's Playbook

Fake • 4.1 Dive

Desc. Line goes away from play to fake out D. Line. Jeff goes up middle

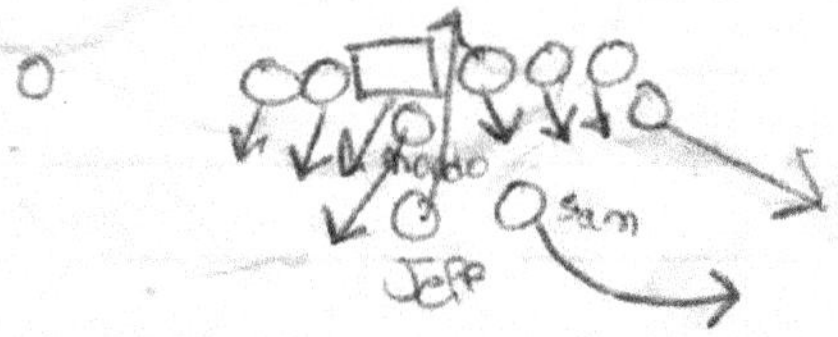

O.G. Pass

Line does regular pass blocking except O.G. who does a down & In.

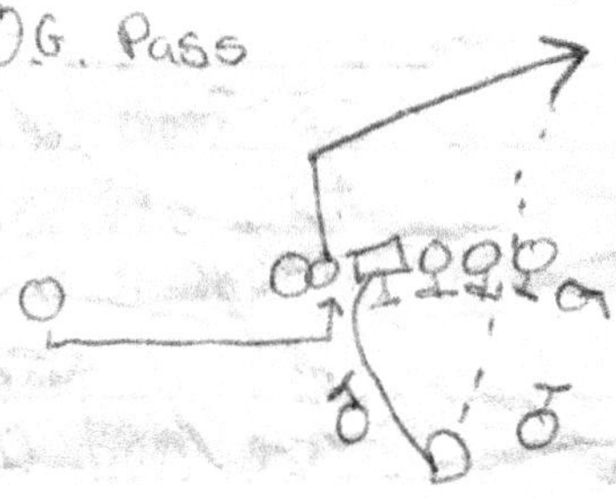

Fake middle Screen

Everybody does middle screen except Jeff who does left screen.

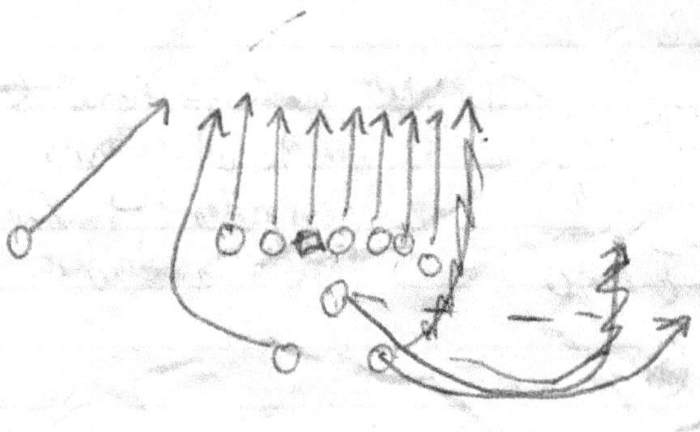

Onside Punt

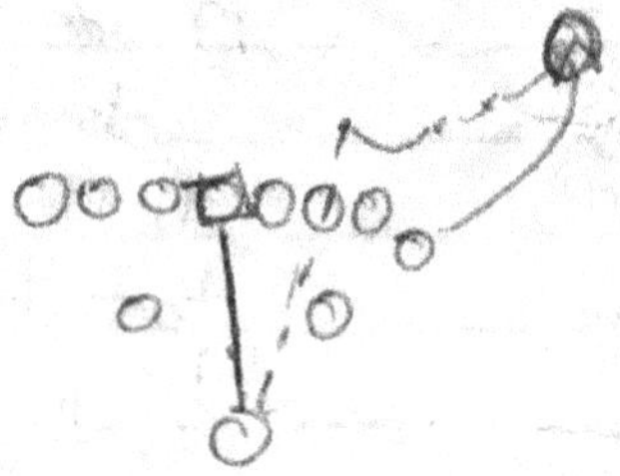

QuickPitch FieldGoal

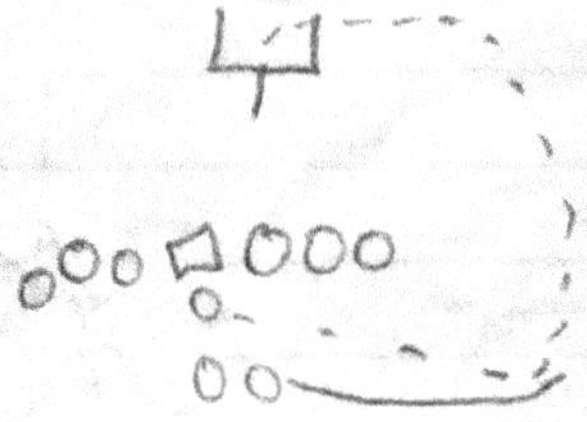

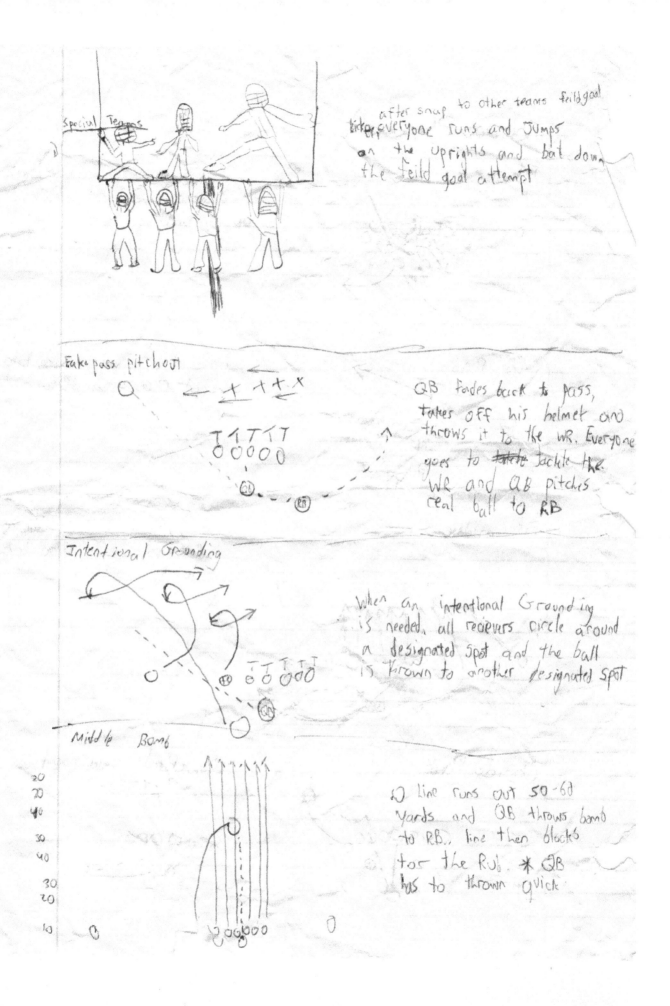

Special Teams

kicker / after snap to other teams feild goal everyone runs and Jumps on the uprights and bat down the feild goal attempt

Fake pass pitchout

QB fades back to pass, takes off his helmet and throws it to the WR. Everyone goes to ~~tackle~~ tackle the WR and QB pitches real ball to RB

Intentional Grounding

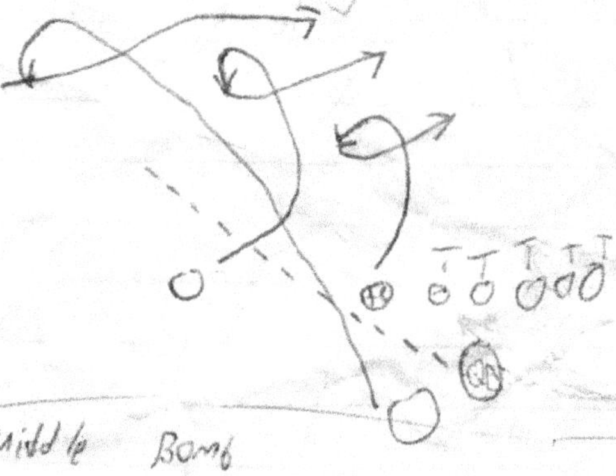

When an intentional Grounding is needed, all recievers circle around a designated spot and the ball is trown to another designated spot

Middle Bomb

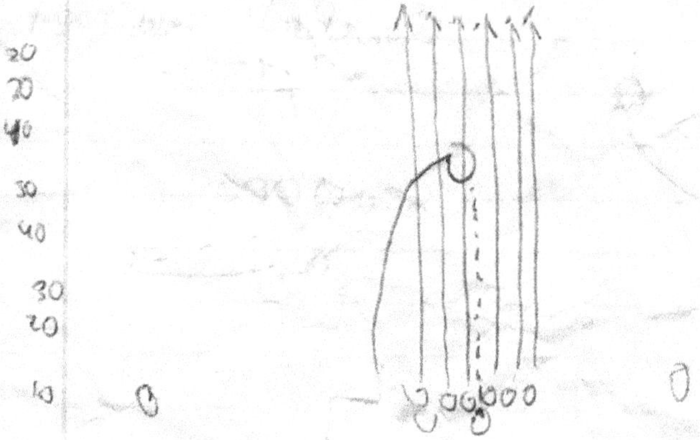

O line runs out 50-60 yards and QB throws bomb to RB.. line then blocks for the RB. * QB has to thrown quick

Console $55.00 (console has no paddles)

Adventure	$10.00
Air-Sea Battle	$5.00
Asteroids	$10.00
Barnstorming	$10.00
* Basic Programming (Keyboard Controllers not included)	$10.00
Bowling	$5.00
Breakaway IV (Breakout)	$10.00
Canyon Bomber	$5.00
Combat (comes with console)	$5.00
Cosmic Ark	$15.00
* Donkey Kong	$15.00
Demons to Diamonds	$10.00
Freeway	$10.00
Gangster Alley	$10.00
* Golf	$5.00
Gunslinger (Outlaw)	$5.00
* Home run	$5.00
Indy 500 (Driving Controllers not included)	$10.00
Maze (Slot racers)	$5.00
Maze Craze	$10.00
Missle Command	$10.00

Night Driver	$10.00
Shark Attack	$15.00
Skiing	$10.00
⊖ Space Combat (Spacewar)	$5.00
Space Invaders	$10.00
Space Jockey	$10.00
⊖ Space war (Space Combat)	$5.00
Speedway II (Streetracer)	$5.00
Stampede	$10.00
Starship	$5.00
Submarine Commander	$5.00
Superman	$10.00
* Surround	$5.00
21 Video Olympics	$10.00
Video Pinball	$10.00

* comes with instructions and box)
⊖ two seperate cartridges (same game)

6-1-88

Jimmy,

Listen first of all You didnt break up with me it was very mutual. I dont want you to end your life dont be stupid. You know I wouldnt want you to kill yourself. O.K be serious now Im in French & I cant write much or I'll get caught by her & I'll get in trouble. I dont know what to write now. b-cos I got to writeback to your letter and I cant find it now. I'll give you your other letter later on. its at my house in my SS. book but I told you that story already. I just got back my French test I got a 53, Good Right! I wish I could find your letter in my shit notebook but I cant so I better go.

Later

W/B Love Me (Kelli)

AED

2/21/85

Lizette,

See I used to go with Louie and he did something to me and we had intercorse (sexual rape). Thats what he did to me and so I had the cops on him and private detectives and my own counselor. I still have the cops on him But me + Louie still talk (undercover). Ray don't want me too but. I can't help it. I was so in love with Louie. Put it like this we were in love we went with each other for 7 months. But I had every thing. But we had to break up from what he did. (Sexual rape). that's why my mom don't let me go out. She's afraid that he might do it to me again. write back

Kenny

1/6/84

Hey moe, whats up? So how ya doin? Its 4th period and its spanish. ¡BORING! I was thinking of you so I figured I'd write. What do you want to do tonight? I don't care what we do as long as Im with you. This teacher is a real head case a real winner. She is about 5 ft. nothing and HUGE! shes wearing this long black blouse with orange flowers. She looks like a garden bed. She has about 5 stories a day. This women could write a 5,000 pg. book with new editions every year. Well enough about her. Poor Stacy she can't go out tonight. She won't be able to see Jerry. Darlene is punished this weekend. She can go out today till 6. Im not sure. But thats life. anyway so whats new? anything

Digital Photography
After School Begins 2/26-27
2:30-4:30 Wednesday
2:30-4:30 Thursday
March Due- 23rd
Photo series - on your Photographer - at least 5 photos
presentation -
google Slides -
Artist presentation
Example of Artist
Talk about how

interesting? nothin much with me just the usual you know.
Well I gotta go cause the bells gonna ring.

See ya later.

Love Ya!
Patricia

Roy 8
= = 24
Darlene 83

stacy
LVS
Jerry

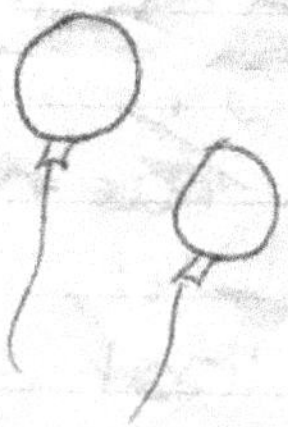

Patricia 11
12
Kenny 83

abdul

Didn't come out to good.

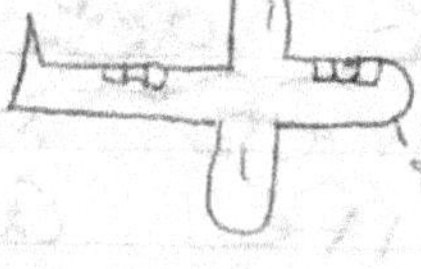

Let me help

HELP? I wish.
Don't worry about it
I'm better off alone.
friends only fuck
me over no offense.
It's just me I guess
not them. I'm an
annoying person you
must admit

EWE! Fuck you
Friends are to share.
I like worrying about
my friends. I like not
having to - but if there
is something to worry
about - it's better to
share it with someone →

1-31-87

My dearest sexy,

hiya loverboy. what's up? not much here. It's 7:34pm I got home about an hour ago but I wasn't allowed to ~~mo~~ make any phone calls. So how are you? I'm okay I guess, I would be better if I could see you. I miss you so much it aint funny. I didn't think it would bother me, you know, not seeing you for 2 days and all, but it does. I miss you, your smile, your hands, being in your arms & most of all, the fun we have when we're together. We have something special and I don't want to lose it. You're like my other half. I don't know what I'd do without you. You are definitely the best thing that ever happened to me. I love you so much. I've been reading your letters and thinking about you. I've never been so happy. I feel as if we've been together forever. I hope that's how long we last. Always-&-Forever. That →

would make me so happy. Who knows? maybe the next wedding we go to together will be ours. You never know. I guess I should stop talking like this to you. You might think I'm getting to serious & break up with me. Who knows? I want you to know that I'll never break up with you. I love you to much to do that or to cheat on you! why cheat on someone when they're all you've ever wanted? I don't need anyone else. I never will. Do you believe me when I tell you I love you? I hope so because it's the truth. I'll be back in a while you just called. hi I'm back. I just got off the phone with you. When I told you I'd explain my reason I wasn't lying. My reason for saying no is partly because I'm afraid of getting pregnant and partly because I'm afraid that you'll break up with me the next day. I know you say you won't but you have to understand, I've been

hurt to many times to take chances
Im not saying you're going to
hurt me, but I want to be sure.
Can you understand? I hope
so. I love you, so if making love
will make you happy Im willing. I
agree with you that it would
show how much we love each other.
When you do it just for the hell
of it it's Fucking - when you do it
out of love its making love. Do you
agree? I consider it making love between
us. Do you. Well let me go before I
cry. I love you & Love

Always
-E-
Forever
Your
"Angel"

P.S. I love You.
P.P.S. I need You.
P.P.S. I want You.
P.P.P.S. I want to ride You.
P.P.P.P.S. I'll never leave You.

al
wa
ys

Nick ♡ Kim

12
28
87

"Always-E-Forever"
"Endless Love"

Sue, 4/25

Hey what's up buddy? Nothing here. I'm
tired. The situation between my parents and
Mark is fucked up. My life really sucks at this
point! I can't believe my mother found out that
he had his own apartment! I'm just so happy
that Mark understands and is hanging in there.
I really think I love him. I mean I never
experienced it. But the way I feel for him, I
do love him and I hope everything work out
for the best of it. I hope you understand me!
Anyway. So when are we gonna hang out?
Just tell me the time, place, + day and I'll be
there. So how's Nicky? I have a bad stomach
ache! Hi, now it's the 26th. Sorry I
didn't finish yesterday but I'm so busy with
tests and everything. Anyway guess what happen
last night. Give-up. Mark broke-up w/ me because
he couldn't deal w/ my mother anymore. But my
friend Jennifer got us back together. I love him
soooo much. When he broke-up w/ me because
of my mother I was gonna Kill her. I
will hate my mother for that! Mark said
he still likes me but he can't deal w/ my
mother anymore. Thank god I'm back w/ him.
Well let me go.

W/B.

Love ya
Lynne.

Lynne 12 — Susan 5
-N- 31 — -N- 22
Mark 84. — Nicky 83. ↖ right?

Notes

Heath Careers

Its my
mind and
no-one comes IN
nobody comes in
Damaged my damaged
no-body come's in
stay out

If I leave
her tomarrow
would still Remember
Me

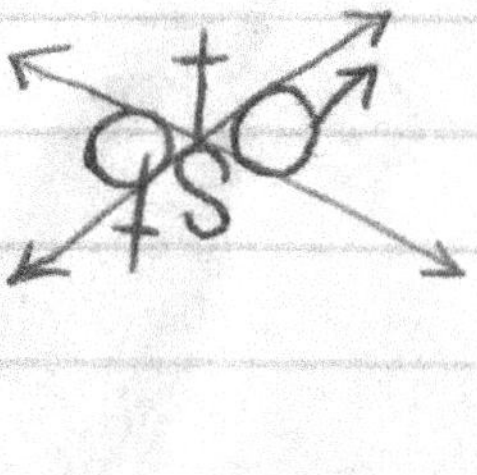

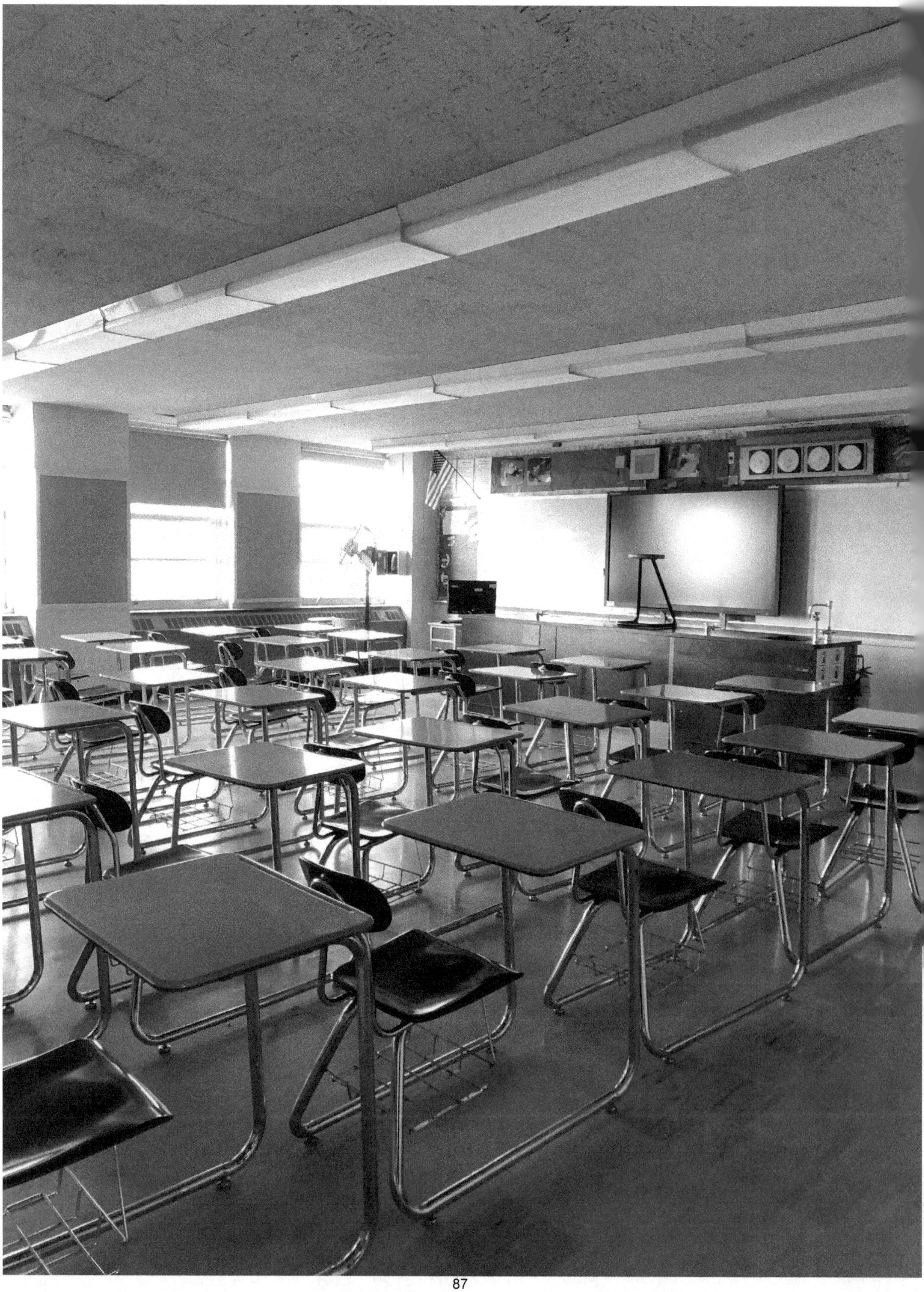

Help

a mad scienti[st]
has given me a
drug

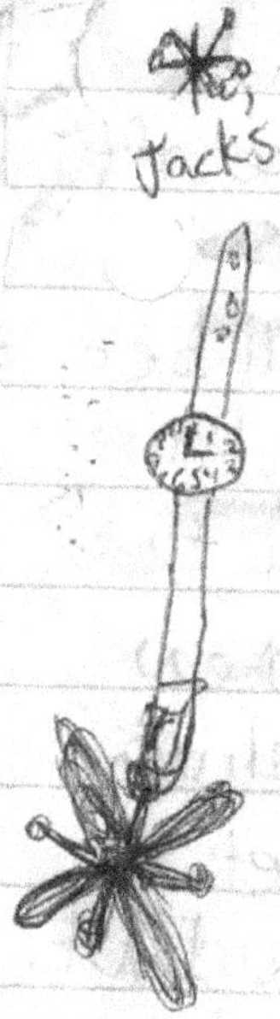

Hi Beth,

I ripped this sheet, so I didn't want to waste it, so I wrote on it. O.K. Now that I told you that, I feel stupid, I don't want to go back to that assholic place. Oh well, no use. Next time I'll throw the chair at him. Enough of getting upset & not saying anything. I'll throw the fuckin' chair at him. Stop! I hate this class. What a SAP!?!, I don't care anymore. I'm not gonna let them get to me. No more! I [illegible] a mad. I need a [illegible]ette to

Oh no
15 more
minutes
left.
I can't
Stand it.
Someone
has the
pass
out.

smoke. I'm going to fade away, I can't, too mad. I wanna go home, take off this uniform & leave the show & I'm waiting in this cell because I have to know. Have I been guilty all this time? Don't you hate when someone has a helium balloon & they let it fly away by accident. That annoys me. The balloon just floats up in the air.

I wish I could be free. I feel caged up like an animal. I wish I could be a bird, cause I could fly away. But it doesn't matter, [illegible] mire to me. [illegible]

Alsover, Me and Brian are over. I'm sad but I'm not gonna cry about it. I had fun while it lasted and thats as far as it goes. We walk in his house and he sat on his dresser and I walk over to him and he pulled me closer and we started kissing. Well then we were on his brm floor. and we were kissing again, he was on top of me and all shit like that And I wanted to talk to him about Linda and he wouldn't. Well we were kissing again and he started to get hard. I felt it because he was holding close and his pants were bulging. Then we went for a walk came back and he took me to the roof and I walked down and we went back to his apartment and we were kissing and he got hard again and then he

tried to go down my pants.
He isn't even going out with me
or seeing me. Then I put my
hands in the way, and I went
home a 1/2 after that. He's such
a reject

Debbie Why didn't you want him to
go down your pants. Did you feel
bad because you weren't going
out with him?... When did
he deny it?...
Anyway I've known
Brian for a long time and his
~~sex~~ reputation is shot to HELL!
Oh Well, I'm glad he didn't
get far with you... I knew you
could handle yourself - Good Girl!
W/B/W Love
Linda

Because he is going out with
Linda he's got a rep and I
would too. He's immature and
he doesn't care for me. What do
they say about him. I felt or I would
feel used because he's going out
with someone who I'm friends with.
he said last night that he didn't a

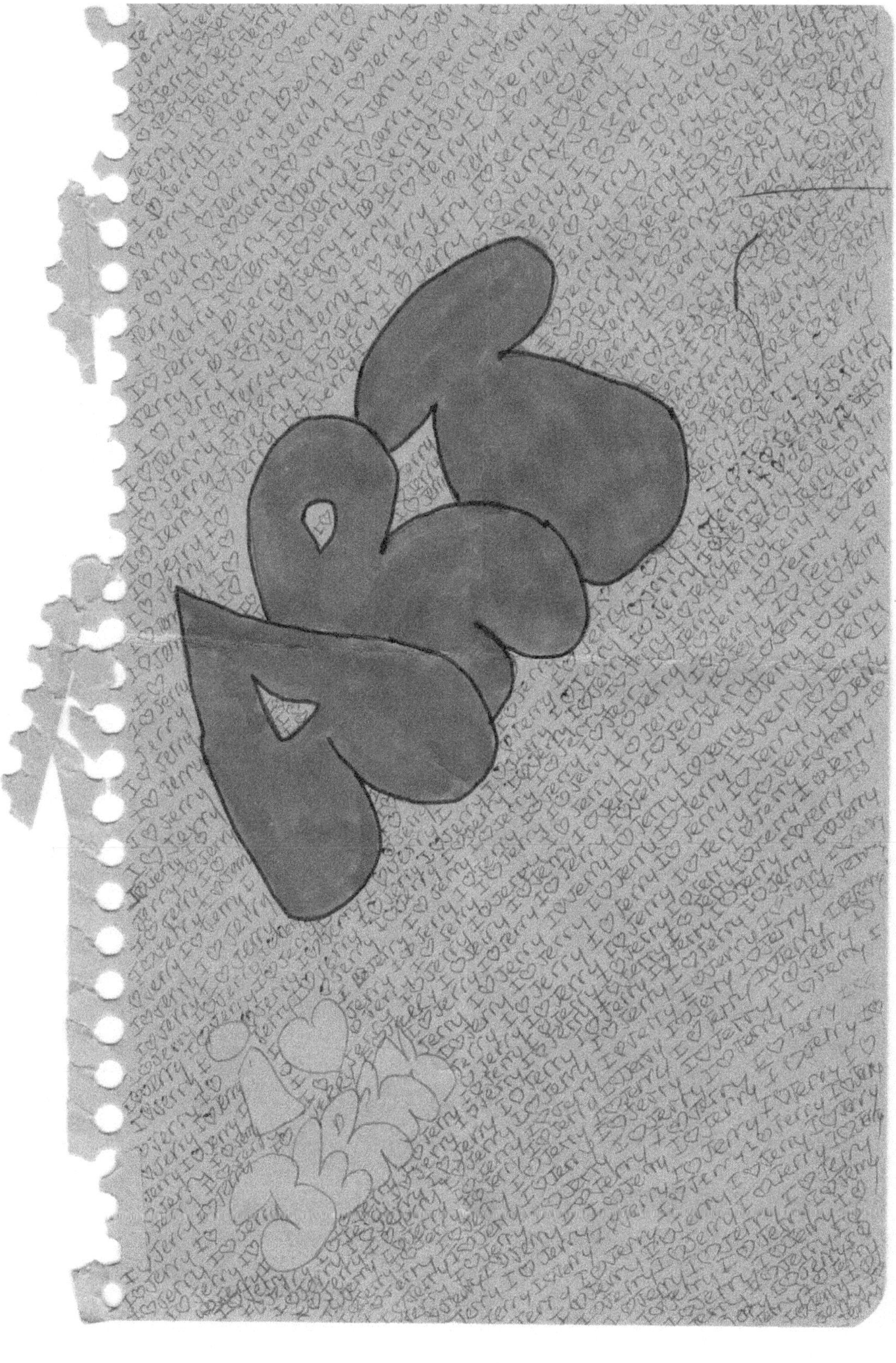

5/01/86

Dear Joel,

So did you like my letter? I know I'm still not very talkative, at least this letter doesn't have any flowers on the bottom of the paper. I have another sub so I decided to write to you, again.

You almost made me cry before. Don't ask me why I'm just depressed and I told you all the reasons why.

So you didn't tell me ~~[illegible]~~ if you like my letter or not. I really am sorry about what happened yesterday, but I guess it was both our faults. Well anyway I am sorry. It's just that a lot of things just depress me. Don't ask me why they just do.

Can you just answer one question? Do you forgive me? I really am sorry. From now on I'll be like you want me. I'll do ~~[illegible]~~ what you want me to, so this way you won't be mad at me for anything anymore. Anyway do you forgive me?

Love Always,

Jennifer

MY
1) GRADE
"A" STICKER
PERSON

Dearest Julietta

Boy are you ~~gon~~ gonna kill me for calling you that!! He he he OK I don't know what happened to all the people at our old lunch table but here's a rundown of everybody's situation

Glenn
Julie } still friends
Mary

Sandy - still skinny fighting with Halia.
Anthony - still overweight fighting with Halia, Sandy etc. etc. (what else is new)
Jarad - extremly obnoxious. Still resembles a goat
Halia - hates all of us finds us very boring people. Well she is a @!?*@. translation: Bitch

So how did your fight go with what's her name (I don't know how to spell it) Try to do me a favor. See if you can find a picture of Loretta from her party because I'm almost positive her hair was brown.

Let's see I know that your still angry about the way I

Started this letter so I'll start again (GASP.)

Dear Julie

There thats better right. I remember that you hate to be called that so I take it back

↑ static

Excuse me while I adjust the fine tuner

There that's better. So if Loretta comes to Wagner next year I'll have to lay down a few rules

① No wrestling Saturday you and her must have fought 3 or 4 times and it was getting interesting because I wanted to fight the winner.

② No singing "Like A Virgin" I mean no singing the song "Like A Virgin" not no singing like a virgin would sing.

③ No doing wheat germ on school premises.

④ No crying if you don't get lunch together.

WAGNER HEROS
LANE
61
BILCHER
68

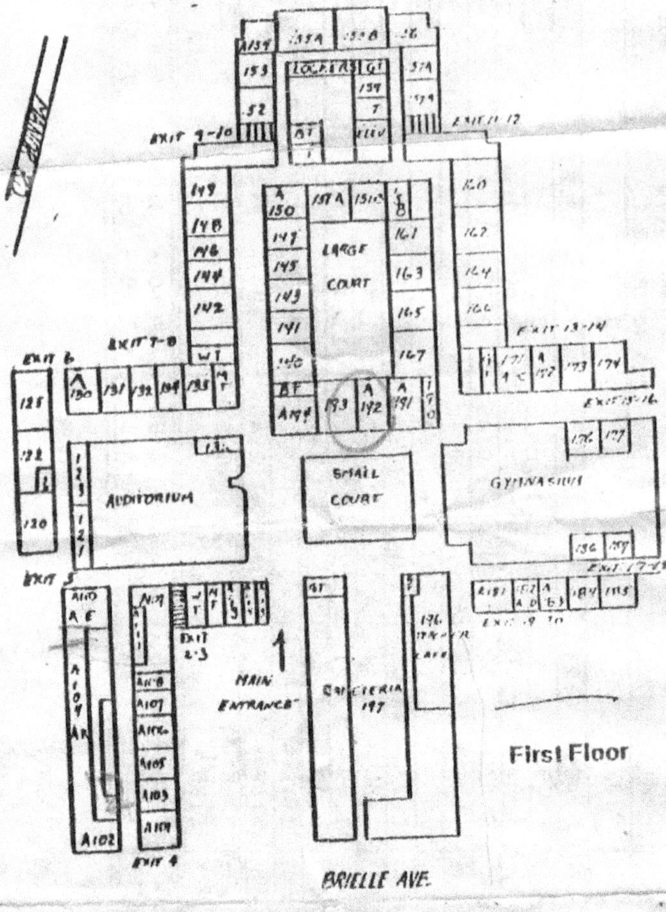

WAGNER FLOOR PLAN

- 18 -

Lisa, 12/13/84

Hi, how's life?
mine's pretty good.
everything with Tommy
is nice right now. He told
me again that I'm getting
my ADB next week & also
called me last night &
told me. So maybe I'm
not going to do anything
else with him for a
while. I'll see if he lives
up to his promises & how
will we get along.

I'm starting not
to give a shit about school.
I get what I get. my average
is 88 so what. I'm used
to 90's but I'm not in
junior high anymore.
I can still get into a
good college & be whatever
I want. Probably a nurse.

So how's Mady? I
hope things work out. I
know how much you like
him. Has Matt told
him about Joanne?
That is such a pissa!

HOKE PAVI
DONATED BY
ROBERT HOKE
WAGNER
SPARTANS
FOOTBALL

I always thought she was miss faithful.

Mechelle is "definitely" getting her abortion next Tues or Wed. If she doesn't get it by then, She's really in for it. I hope that would never happen to me. But I would be smart enough to be careful.

I hope I go to October's tomorrow night. I loved the Ultimate. I can't handle disco guiders anymore. They make me so sick. I love every-thing about rock. I love the way rockers look, act dress, etc. It is so great.

Well, the bell is about to ring.

Love ya lots!
Marianne
Best friends forever!

Rich
I don't feel very good.
"It's that time of the month"
you know what I mean.
And my stomach hurts. But
I'll just look at you, & I'll
forget all about the pain.
I hope she comes home
really late Friday night.
God, you have no idea what
I feel like doing right
now. You're such a fox
Rich. W/B to me ok?
Love
Diane

If it's that time you can't do anything or
can you? I don't know about those things.
I hope I can get away Friday nite.
So are you gonna tell me the rest of what your
thinking? W/B ~~Love~~ Richie

Well, it would be pretty
messy wouldn't it? I hope
you can get away too. To be forward with you I feel like
doing everything you can imag →

them pills I take
make me feel sick
I want to throw
up and some I
do and I hope
I not the
victim that
the pills dont
agree with
be cause
their not
100%
proof
that
they won't
get you
pregnant

Wendy,

Hi! whats up?! not much here. I really ~~this~~ dont like that kid, I dont know why I said I did. He is a little cute but I really dont like him. I am not just saying this so you wont say anything ~~or~~ to him or to that girl, Lisa. I just dont really like him! Honest! I ~~just~~ saw Jeff going 3rd and he blushed when he saw me and gave a little "hi" without even opening his mouth. I dont want him to think I hate him so I said "Hi, whats up" & smiled at him. I dont care what anyone says I think he likes & just wont say anything because of his friends. I hate him for the way he is * cause if he wasnt like that then maybe he would say something. I still really like and always will even if he dont like. I wish he did, everything I want I always never get it. I like to walk down a hall + punch every ~~g~~ ugly + fat girl with pimpley + greasy hair with ankle bracelets + some gorgeous guy on her arm. They get me sick. Maybe we should pig out everyday until we weigh at least 290 lbs., never ~~wash our faces~~, so we get very bad acne, never wash our hair ~~so~~, so it comes really greasy + never wear makeup + then maybe we'll get somewhere in life. Do you want to go Bike riding today I'll call at 5:30

Love ya
Chris
Chris
[illegible]
[illegible]
Steff

Shari,

A stranger is watching! I hope somebody like Kenny didn't do it, now I don't know who I can trust. Just about 10 minutes before we discovered what happened I was in Chick's house. The little girl I babysit for was selling candy so I brought her there. His mother actually bought, she is such a sweetheart! I feel so sick! I was walking all around N.Y. and it was cold yesterday, I think that's why I'm sick. That perverted guy wants Liz to go out with him! She told him he was too experienced. He asked her if he could teach her! Oh, my god! On Sat. when I was at the Mall, some guy flipped out from a drug overdose. It was so scary, he was wacked off his butt!

W/B/S Love

Ronni (Vito)

DEAR JESS

I TELL YA I'LL TRY MY BEST TO STOP BY WHAT A DICK I AM I SHOULD HAVE CHECKED WITH BEFORE I MADE PLANS. I'LL TELL I'D FUCKEN RATHER BE WITH YOU I HOPE YOU KNOW IT BUT THERE DEPENDING ON ME TO BE THERE I CANT BAG THEM YA KNOW. I'D BEEN WANTING TO GET TOGETHER JUST ME AND YOU FOR A LONG TIME BUT THINGS JUST DIDNT FALL IN PLACE. THEY WILL SOMEDAY REMEMBER I'M GAME IF YOUR GAME. YA KNOW A LOT OF PEOPLE HAVE BEEN SAYING THAT ~~MY~~ I HAVE A BAD ATTITUDE AND IT SUX. ANOTHER THING I ALWAYS LOOKED DEPRESSED EVEN IF I'M ~~B~~ IN A GOOD MOOD I LOOKED DEPRESSED, I DONT KNOW WHY IT JUST GOES THAT WAY I GOT MY HAIR CUT FOR REALLY NO DAMN REASON I REALLY DIDNT WANT IT CUT BUT I DID IT ANYWAY IT SEEMED LIKE THE RIGHT THING AT THE RIGHT TIME. YOU SEE THAT'S HOW MY MIND WORKS, ANOTHER THING GO FOR IT WITH THE WEIGHT

Always
BRUNO
Mötley Crüe
IRON
MAIDEN

Dear Jana

Are you running for any of the sing offices. If you are which one are you running for.

w/l/p [signature]

Danny told me to run for chorus director but I'm going to if I'm a director then I can't really be in the show (like on stage) what about you?

Tanya

I'm afraid if I run for an office I won't be able to try for a major stage role (role). I have alot of excellent ideas that I've seen from other sings in brooklyn who are 30 yrs ahead of our sings in experience. If we can model our sing like theirs were garanteed (how ever you spell it.) to win I saw both junior & senior sing here & Sheepsed H.S. Sophmore

Sing blew them both away.

[illegible]

If you try out - you'll definately get a part + you could also run for director or something & still be in the show. Sonia Maria (Maria's sister) did that. She had a part + was our over all director. But even if you don't run for director or anything you can still submit any ideas you have to our advisor (+ for all we know it could be Ranny!) Besides it doesn't really matter if the sophmores win or not as long as were good - I mean GREAT!!!

If we can take ideas that have worked and won for 30 yrs instead of constantly trying to be origanal, we'll be great. Even though if we werent origanal no one would accept us.

Toni Ann Loves Jimmy

Michele Loves Paul 10/17/84

Dear Toni Ann,

Hi! How are you? I might go to long Island this weekend. I'm supposed to go to a party tonight but I have to work. Did Jimmy get a job yet? How are you & him getting along. I'm in-love. Today is 1 month-1 week 2 Days.

Write Back Now!

Love,

? (Burnout)

Dear Michele,

Hi, I am fine, and how are you. This weekend I ~~an~~ am not doing anything great th weekend. Me & Jimmy getting along O.K. but last night we had a fight & break up. But we got ~~back~~ back. How is Paul That good that you ar

in love. what does he
look like? You never
told me. I what to get
high ~~tod~~ tonight.

Love,
Me

BYI
see you
Monday

Dori Ann 3
-Loves- 30
Jimmy 81
forever.

Michele
-Loves-
Paul
forever

Camille, 12-23-82

hi! how are you? I'm fine I guess. Are you going tonite? I don't think I am. Sorry I was in a bad mood again in gym. I don't know what it is I've been confused and I don't know what to do about it. Listen here Camille I ~~except~~ expect to hear a phone call from you over vacation. Don't worry Tommy might not even wanna go tonite so don't get your blood pressure all upset for nothing. I hope this kid I think is gorgeous goes Tuesday nite. I think I'm in love Naa! I haven't really liked anybody as muched as I liked El Jerko (Frankie) do you know what I mean? you know your right about what you said when your having a great time then someone comes along you don't want to be bothered but when their's no-one you wished there was someone either way you can't win! Oh well that's the brakes This class is beat I had a great time in Math. If you see your cousin that knows Gerard find out if Gerard say's anything bad about me. Gerard's a jerk he got me so sick that's why I broke up with him. He thought he was God's gift to boys. What a jerk. So did

Tommy tell you what he got
you. Imagine if it's an
ankle braclet you better
shove it in Billy + Joe's face.
I would love to see their
face. Well listen I gotta
go.

Love You
Susan

P.S.
tell Guy I understand
that his fingers may
be broken But I wish
him a Merry Christmas
and Happy New Year anyway.

AL Camille 10 Tommy 4
WA loves 31 loves EV
YS Tommy 82 Camille ER

Susan
♡loves♡
NO-ONE
(For The Time Being)

P.S.S.
call me!
[redacted]
don't forget!

10-29-86

Michele

Hi! what's up? Not much here. Did you get caught yet. Shit I don't feel good. What are you gonna do about Chris? Do you still love him? I asked Joe in his letter what he was doing this weekend? Do you wont to go to the city it would be fun. I have to get off this fuckin boring Island.. If your wondering who I'm going out with its no one. Remember that kid Anthony well he's an asshole ya know. I must of said hi 3x & he didn't say anything back (Dick). Michele I want a boyfriend Bad. Can you sugest anyone

well let me go my
fuckin hand hurts.

Bye
Love ya

Renea (WB)

Nicole

Cort
YAMAHA
MUSCI MAN

Cooper,

St. Johns is on fire. They have the blessing of the Pope, and Reagan. God bless the Redmen Hell have the Hoyas.

Chris Mullin - AP player of the year.
Bill Wennington - 2nd team All-America, Canadian Olympic star.
Willie Glass - high Jump.
Mike Moses: 2nd in steals, Best play maker in Big East. WRONG - MICHAEL ADAMS
Walt Berry - Superstar - Next year
NOTE - Mullin Carries the team.

MICHAEL JACKSON
Gary McLAIN
Dwayne WASHINGTON

~~Bench~~ STILLO
M. Jackson - 6'7" point guard. is slick
R. Stewart - good back up to wennington.
S. Jones - speed, not proven yet!!

St Johns the beast of the East!!!
Georgetown the Least of the East!!

St Johns. 74

Georgetown 69

St Johns hits from the outside and bangs the boards. Ewing stays out of foul trouble and slows down the offense (which is a plus to St Johns)

Love Ya

See you at Kentucky - vs - Villanova

Georgetown had a hardgame last time, but a good rest has helped. St. Johns hasn't clicked yet. but there due. Georgetown has the experience and motivation. StJohns will make it close. Take Georgetown to win StJohns with the points.

I Agree. St. John's might be due, But tell me: Did THEY FACE AN opponent of G'town's caliber OUT West? Nope! Opinion: I think Ga Tech could have beat St. JOHN'S. With A healthy Duane Ferrell, THEY WOULD HAVE BEAT GeorgetowN!

Cooper

CBS Scorecard

StJohns 74 Georgetown 69
Willianova 80 memphis St. 76

Mullin 30 points 10-12 shooting
6-6 from line. 12 rebounds.
11 Assists. 5 steals. 1 Block shot
Named mvp.

No! No! No!

G'towN by 5 (OT)
'Nova by 2 (buzzer-beater.)

Rock (G'town)
Rock G'TOWN
ROCK G'TOWN

When did he say ~~that~~ he didn't want to get involved? Did you ask him if he was going out with her?

He told her at Great Adventure is over with the two of them?

I asked him did you ever goo with her? and he said what do you mean and I said did you go with her? and he said go where? What a jerk I started laughing I couldn't help it & I said did you kiss her and he felt like a dick and said I don't know & He is an unexperienced fool & He probably didn't want to get involved cause he didn't know what to do!

He was only putten on a big act! He was trying to make you feel sorry for him! He dropped her because he loves you! (Only joking) That girl that sits next to you, Did I make her start crying Thursday when I said she needed a shave? Bye the way she looks like she did shave the hair off of her face!

I didn't know you said that to her but it dosen't look like she shaved she's still hairy!

Not as much as last week! I was trying to make Laird remember what I did to that girl and then she started looking at me + him! He still didn't know what I was saying! He's a big shit!

I know he's a big shit! but she's not that bad, a little hairy but nice! You should shave that mustache you've got! You should think harder.

FUCK YOU STUPID! I DON'T HAVE A MUSTACHE AND IF I DO (All girls DO) It's BECAUSE of MY ITALION HERITAGE AND I'M PROUD OF IT

My mustache is still growing in! (I HOPE) I was only jokin about your mustache! You dont have one! I WAS ONLY KIDDING too YOU KNOW I DIDN'T MEAN IT But I AM PROUD OF MY HERITAGE Well so am I so

Hi Beth,

This is the 2nd letter on the ripped sheet. It wasn't my fault. It was yours. It's going to RAIN. good. I see danger.

Warning

Poisonous

X Don't listen to me anymore.

No! No! No!

I don't know what to write. Get smashed. I want a bottle of Vodka. I want to drink. I want to get smashed. Yesterday, Patty saw Keith Louis & Jack at the college talking to little Jeanie. Keith said he's thinking about going to college. Ha! that's funny.

I smell chocolate.
Want some Now!
How do you like spainish.
Ha, NO, NO, NO.
I am tired. Are you
going to school tomorrow?
I don't want to go, but I
will.

Don't!

Do it!

starburst
starburst orange
Starburst Starburst
starburst
starburst
orange starburst
Starburst orange
Starburst
orange starburst
Starburst
orange
Starb

Hi back again
Normal condition.
Detination, termination.
I'll have to leave now
Read this when your
bored. This is boring. Nothing
more to say so I'll say
goodbye for the last time.

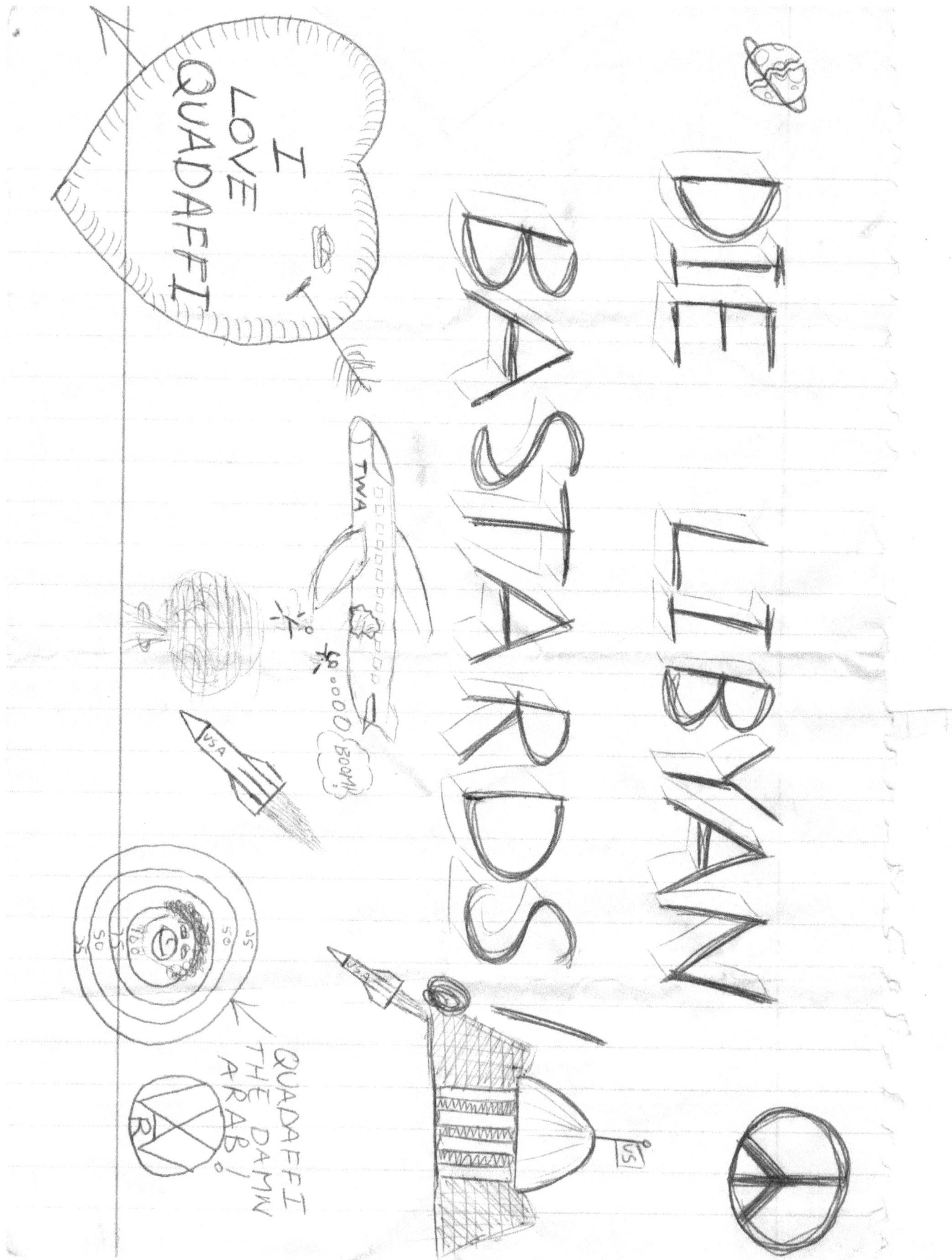
DIE LIBYAN
BASTARDS!
I LOVE QUADAFFI
TWA
BOOM!
USA
USA
US
QUADAFFI THE DAMN ARAB!

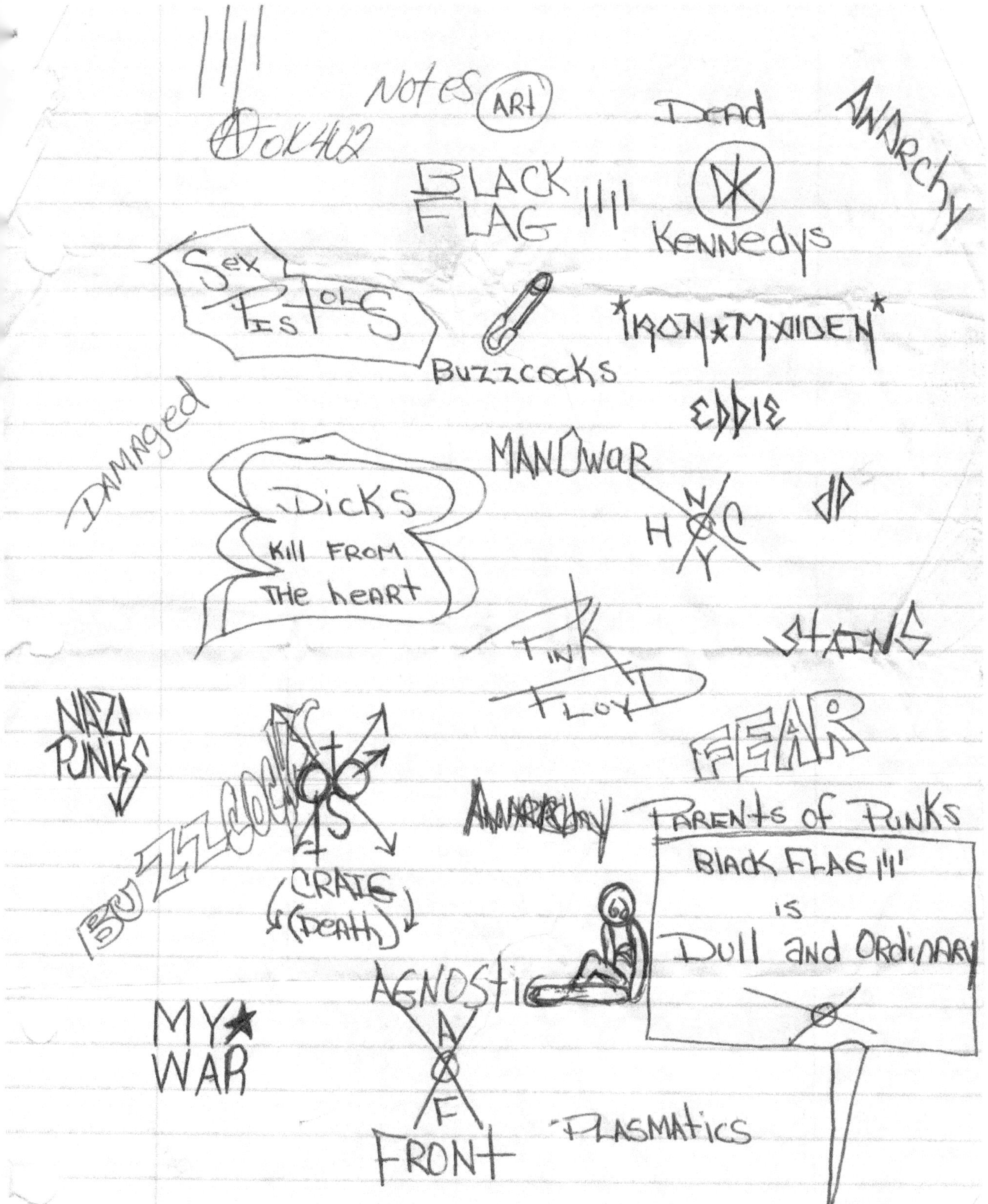
Notes
ART
Dead Kennedys
ANARchy
BLACK FLAG
Sex Pistols
Buzzcocks
IRON MAIDEN
EDDIE
Damaged
MANOWaR
DicKS
Kill FROM THE heart
NYHC
STAINS
Pink Floyd
FEAR
NAZI PUNKS
BUZZCOCKS
CRAIG
(Death)
Parents of Punks
BLACK FLAG
is
Dull and Ordinary
AGNOSTIC
FRONT
MY WAR
PLASMATICS

Don't Throw It All Away!!

Here we go
breaking off what we have built
leaving out
All the good things that we felt
Where was I?
Where was I before you came
cause ~~the~~ from the first time
that I saw you, I knew
that maybe I
Maybe I'd do something wrong
oh, but how I ~~t~~ tried
but the words won't fit
the song
I found the door
but I couldn't find the key
cause from the first time that
I saw you, I knew, you were
made for me
-So don't throw it all away
cause I don't want to be the
one who's gonna hafta
beg you to stay
and I don't want be the
one to change your mind
one more time, please stay
don't throw it all away
So it seems, I'm just taking
out on you, don't you

know, only you can see
through
I found the door, now I
know that your the key
cause from the first time
that I saw you I knew
You were made for me...
So don't
throw it all away!!

Lori,

Hi whats up? Nothing much here I have a sub I'm so.... stupid I could have went to 5th lunch to see John but I didn't know there was a sub and now its too late So I can't believe that letter I think Tina will. I just saw Allison and she said that Frank's putting Tina's name on his car, I can't believe Tara is mad at you. She gets mad over the stupidest things. John + Frank have the whole summer planned. We're going to Great Adventure + the Beach. Like I just might put on a bathing suit while John's there. I hope we don't go I'll feel so stupid. I can't wait to get back to the woods at least we had something to do and we all had fun hangin out now all we do is go to movies + mall There's nothing else

for us to do I hope it gets warmer that way we'll have 3 things that we cards on weekends instead of just 2. What did you and Nicole do friday night? The movie wasn't great so you didn't miss much. Do you think Frank really likes Tina or is he just saying all that to get what he wants (if you know what I mean) She really likes him a lot though. Do you think Frank will go to the woods if he does do you think allison will want to go. I gotta go. W/B

Danielle

Sorry
Sloppy

You

4-19-83

Dear Paul

hi how are you? im doing pretty good. So whats up? not much here. Franca saiphi! I feel so stupid writing you a letter when Lisa told me you wanted me to write you a letter I figured "no problem" this is going to be really easy, but I dont know where to start or what to really write. Well first of all I didnt mean to walk away from you friday night but I felt really stupid plus Mike just left us standing there like 2 jerks I didnt know what to say so I left. I could have killed him. So hows Tottenville? do you like it there or do you like Wagner better? Did you have fun at the party? It was pretty good but I wanted to stay later but my mother wouldnt let me she never trusts me. What time did you stay till? Im sick, I cant breathe last week I had swollen glands, this week I sneeze & cough I dont think Im going to make it through this week. I have so much schoolwork I have to do Im getting la[te] and my parents

Dear Jimmy, 4-22-85

Hi! I'm so upset about what you did. I thought you had more respect for me than to fuck around with something as serious as that. Why are you playing head games with me I dont know why you think I'm something to fool with because I'm not about to get played with again. If you want us to work you'd better cut the shit because I'm so very sick of fighting with you over stupid things. You say all I want to do is fuck you when you tell me for a week how guilty you feel. I really don't know why you do this to me. We should have never ever done it & I knew you'd feel [illegible] way. I really dont even think you even [illegible] about me Jimmy because you think I haven't got any feelings. I hope I'm not pregnant because if I am I cant go out with you anymore. As soon as I turned you on you would have pulled out. You promised me you would never do that to me. And you laughed when you were doing it like you wanted me to have the kid. I'll never understand why do you do what you do sometimes I can't figure you out. How do you know you're fertile are you a doctor. I'm scared I

go through with this again I dont have
the nerves for it. Sure you could take care of
it you've got enough troubles of your own and
your going to pay $350 for an abortion.
Its not funny to have to wonder if you
are or your not. I'm debating whether or
not I should give you the note or not.
Is it worth the bother of spilling my
guts out over this. I just want to be left
alone for a while to think.

Forgive me I am
confused,
Lori

Hi Sue,

I haven't talked to you in awhile so I decided to write to you. How was your weekend? What's new with E.P.? On Friday we went driving with Mr. Unger (Older) for the first time. Rhonda went down Manor past the post office and pulled over on a quiet street. Then I got in the front seat. I was kind of nervous about starting. ~~He told me to put on the~~ directional signal to pull out. I put on the windshield wiper by accident! Nancy was teasing me so much on the way home. It was funny for a diz like me.

My dad took me driving on Saturday morning. On Manor Road by David D's street I signaled for a left turn and I made a right turn. The guy in the left lane gave me such a dirty look! With a little practice I should get better. Besides driving and shopping my weekend was pretty boring. Oh yeah, my parents bought me a dress for the Arista Installation. It's light blue and gray pinstripes. This class is dull! W/B

Love, Bethie

Hi Beth-a-do!

How is you? I is fine. I don't like E.P. anymore. I went to my sisters house in Brooklyn this weekend. I left Friday and slept over. Saturday we went shopping. I got a dress too, for Arista. It's black & red vertical stripes on top and the skirt part is black. ~~Saturday night Barbara, Alex, and I met~~ my parents and Bobby & Joanne for dinner at this really nice restaurant in Little Italy. Its called "Il Cortile" or something like that. Yesterday I went to an SAT class and slept all day. I guess I had an o.k. weekend.

It's good that your practicing driving. You'll probally be an expert driver in a couple of weeks. I have faith in you.

Love, Susan

Hi Sue,

How is you, again? That doesn't make sense. So what! That sounds like fun going out with your whole family. I feel bad about Maureen's birthday. I wanted to get her something but I had to buy my mom a present. Her birthday was yesterday. Today after 8th period I'm gonna see Fiddler on the Roof. They're showing the movie to get ideas for the play. I probably won't join the play because I don't have time, but I want to see it! We're going ~~skating on~~ to Motions on Friday. You going? How come you don't like E.P anymore? Me, Terri B, & Sue T are probably going to the city the weekend of the Junior Trip. Why don't you go?

Sorry Sloppy

W/B this class.

Love, Beth

Susan

BETHIE

I'M FAT, RAJ.

Wear
Safety

Kong
'83

9/24/84

Darren,

Sup, How are you?
I hope when you read this you will think of me!
That jerk is still sitting near me. how was your weekend?
Mine was Great!
You know that you have Curly hair?
I just noticed it today.
~~well~~ oh today your wearing jordache jeans, blue shirt with white & tourquise stripes, green underwear & Grey Puma's.
well So long Dude

Love YA

Z

Janine

Z

METAL
kicks
Fuckin
ASS

Z

Heavy
metal
rules

Guidos
&
Glitter's
suck (But
your
ok)

I'm sure your interested →

well your
not a guido
your
a breaker & I can
take breaker's but not
cushines ↙

I can't wait until my husband
comes home I know he probably
mad at me because his mother
wasn't suppose to know that
he was in the hospital he told
me not to tell her and she
took my letter out of my
(snatched it) so I think
he's mad at me if I don't
get a letter this week I
know he is.

write him and
tell him what
happen. Didn't you
hear me calling
you Keith in gym
I said Mrs Long
but I guess you didn't
hear me. So what's up?

no I didn't hear you the last
letter I got from Keith he
said when he comes home
he is going to fuck the
shit out of me but he said
sex me up not I ——— me

HA! HA! HA! I know you can't wait till he comes back. Are you using protection or are you planning to have a kid when he gets back

yes I am because I go in the Marines with him not in it you know just hope it happens if not I'll have 45 or 30 to 60 day for it to happen.

Are you sure you want a kid now. Don't you want to wait. What will your mother say or father.

Are yours planning to get married.

yes we are getting married when ~~we~~ I get to go down after graduation or maybe up here. my mother + father cant say any I am old enough to make my own decisions or maybe minds will change and will wait but if it happens well I dont want to loose the

DAWN, 2/15/85

I'm gonna get right to the point you have a hell of a lot of nerve saying what you said this morning. Now I could have just let it go at that - and it would have been perfect timing because just yesterday I was thinking how I wasn't going to let you or anyone else for that matter make me feel like a fool again. But before I do that I'm gonna set the record straight because I'll be damned if I let you waste a year and a half of my life.

I don't give a shit about you huh, my problem all this time has been that I cared too much - way too much. You're one of the very few people who I do care about and I tried hard to prove it but time and time again you just threw it back in my face. I tried to believe that you cared about me, I made myself crazy thinking about it - all just wasted time. You'd be a great actress though, I just realized what a phony you are. You care only about yourself and everyone else is just there for you to use and shit on. I've taken more than my share of shit from you.

I thought you understood me, you understand shit, you think what you want and that's that. You said you would have killed for your grandfather, well I would have killed for you. I spent my 17th birthday crying because I thought I had lost you-my best friend what a fool I've been But you must have had a lot of good times laughing about it though Good, I'm really glad.

It took so long for me to accept the fact that I needed someone - you I don't need you - I can go up to anyone and ask ~~them to make me feel like shit~~

You've past a few comments lately as to my "always being in your business" well I can take care of that. What Dawn wants, Dawn gets so I'll do one better than just stay out of your business - I'll stay out of your life completely. Now that should make you happy - or maybe not. but I'm sure you'll find someone else to use, in no time at all.

Thanks for everything anyway
good + bad

Melissa

THAN All of US
Every Guidos
Physical attraction
Brooklyn Girls
Rock
Madonna
Nammie
John
DA House!!
Shannon
Disco Rules!
B Funhouse
Wagner Boosters #1
Rocks!
(Angel) Eyes
Tisha & Kammy
LET THE Music PLAY!
Holiday
Searchin' Lookin' for Love
Lookin for Love
98.7 Kiss
Madonna #1
Randi Loves Tommy
Sue N Paul
Falcon Football
Disco MAN
FACE it All you Guido's That's All I'm goin' to SAY!

hey Dee
'SUP?
Later for Disco
Joe

Disco, It's not Music
It's A Disease
The symptoms
Are paranoia
Bordeom
constant Brushing of Hair
extremely tight closthes

Rock N Roll
We like this
Music,
Disco, is
Strickly for the
STAY At HOMES

"THE MAN CAnn't Bust our
Music" Disco
yes

Millie,
~~I~~ I cannot understand why your Angry At me AGAIN If it WAS because of our talk last night, this fight is ~~ca~~ uncalled for If your pissed About somthing please have A talk with me About it And we can come with ~~to~~ A ~~n~~ conclusion You got mad over A dump reason, I'll explain this to you if you call me Please Millie I Really Don't understand, I'm trying hard right now ~~know~~ for our relationship to last. It hurt me bad to hear in the back round while I was speaking with your Farther. I heard you say you never wanted to see me AGAIN. I wish you would At least talk to me About it.

We had also made plan's to go out Friday night, ~~W~~ We're supposed to paint the town red, or what ever color's I have Left in my garage. But serious, you say you don't want to see me AGAIN in A million years (or was it A thousand). Does this mean

our Fridays date is off. (Some people say I can't take a hint, I wonder why) - don't stop me now "I'm on a roll," And your supposed to say "I'm Millie." Thank you.

I think every time we fight I become demented. I know if I don't talk to you tonite, I'll attempt suicide - I'll jump off the ~~Brooklyn Bridge~~, make that my dog's doghouse I forgot I'm afraid of heights, or I'll even try somthing worse like cutting my wrist with a banana or another simular object.

Please Millie I'm going crazy, These jokes are terrible, I can't ~~beleive~~ ~~beleave~~ believe your still reading this. - Millee, Please TALK TO ME. JUST FOR A FEW Minutes, Please

Please call me at 6:30 or 10:30 - 11:00 tonite. Thank you very much,

I LOVE YOU

XXXXOOOO Anthony

high Jess, 10/22

What's up? Michelle is a fuckin' asshole! She's going to get a beatin'! My friends Sarah and Laurie are going to kick her ass this weekend. I'm going to tell them what happened today! She's going to get the shit kicked out of her. She's such a skanky bitch! I hate her! Is she in any of your classes? Do you see her in the hallways? She's got a big mouth for a fuckin' wimp. Her mouth is going to get her in a lot of trouble! Anyway, this fuckin' school sux! There's a bunch of fuckin' assholes in this school! I can't take it! I wish there was a school for only cool metalist. That would be so great!

(over)

This school is made up of
3 categories
15 [redacted]% cool people and 5% total itiots
60 [redacted]% stupid guidos + guidettes
20 preppie prick head
Those statistics are pretty
pathetic. I hate this school.
Gimme a fuckin' break. I think
I'm going to die! Well, let
me go before I get carried
away. Talk to ya later. Bye!

Keri

ANGELWITCH IRON MAIDEN

SLAYER

MOTLEY CRUE KISS

Judas Priest OZZY

RATT ANTHRAX

SCORPIONS HELIX

W.A.S.P. DEMON FLIGHT

EXCITER GRYME REAPER

ZEBRA

IRON DOGS ANVIL ALKATRAZ

ACCEPT KICKAXE MOTORHEAD RIOT

WRATHCHILD BLACK SABBATH AC/DC

METALLICA MANOWAR Y&T RAVE[illegible]

GIRLSCHOOL DIO HOLO[illegible]

ARMORED SAINT STEELER VENOM

[illegible]IL FATE QUEENSRYCHE CASH

11/24

To Larry,

I don't want to go out with you anymore, I had just about enough of your bull. Lets just both go our own way because I don't want to ~~get~~ go out with you anymore. And you don't have to worry about me calling you or even saying hello to you anymore because I don't want to. And you don't have to worry about me wanting to go back with you, even if I ever do, I wouldn't put myself to do it again, because I dont want a boyfriend. I am 16 years old & I want freedom. So you go have your fun with your friends & girlfriends and dont say anything to me because if you want to be like that, ~~[illegible]~~. & not talk to me, then go ahead. I had enough of your shit. I'll just pretend I never new you, & dont worry I won't go to motions that much anymore, so ~~I don't~~ have to see you.

Maria.

TARANTO
4
RODRIGUEZ
3
RUFFLER
51

SPARTAN
ONOR ROLL
1976
KARTALIS
GAETA
JONES
LOGUIDICE
RIVERA
RYAN
1977
BACCILIERI
BARACATO
CORRIGAN
DALLAS
DUGAN
McNEIL
MERENDINO
PEDDIE
PIEZCHALA
SCANLON
WILLIAMS
1978
DICKERSON
J.KIELTY
LYNCH
MILITELLO
ORENDER
PICA
SCHMIDT
VALLO-BERA
VALENTINE
WEISNER
1979
BONNAMO
CAMBRIA
CAMMISA
DEMIRKAN
J. PAPE
V. PAPE
REILLY
1980
ALTUCHLER
BELCHER
COLANGELLO
J. FILLIPINI
GUERRA
MONFILETTO
OLSEN
RIVERA
SORENSON
1981
ANTICO
J. BARRY
KITOJNA
RODA
RUDIGER
RYAN
B. ZINK
1982
K. BARRY
BODI
COFFEY
CONLON
ENGELS
V. FILLIPINI
FORSYTH
GIORDANO
HERMENSEN
LINDIE
McCARREN
McINTYRE
MORRIS
OLIVERI
PRICKETT
RICHARDSON
ROMEO
SARCONE
SCARRA
SKIDMORE
STAPLETON
STINSON
1983
ANARUMO
BERNSTEIN
R. CURRAN
GARDA
HANLEY
LAMBIASI
MARTUCCI
PIETRACATELLA
TATE
TEPPER
TROGLIO
M. ZINK
1984
AHLBORN
BASILE
CENCI
G. DIMAURO
GIBERSON
T. GUZZI
HARRELL
ISOLA
LABARCA
LUNDWALL
ROMANO
SEABERG
1985
D. COLEMAN
EDELSTEIN
INNIS
MATHIS
McKAY
E. O'HARE
OLSEN
SALZER
SIMO
VELLA
WOLFE
1986
BROWN
CALABRESE
CHARLES
C. DAI
DICKERSON
L. DIMAURO
GONZALES
HAWKINS
HOLCOMB
HOLTON
JASCO
KANE
T. KIELTY
LASALLE
LA BUE
1986
MARZO
NAGROWSKI
ORLANDO
PRINCE
1987
BOONE
BRAXTON
CALAVETTA
S. COLEMAN
P. DEFILIPPIS
HOERLE
LEVOYER
MARTORANO
McCARTHY
MODENA
O'BRYANT
PATTERSON
F. REALI
SAN - FILLIPPO
SAYERS
SMITH
1988
ABBOTT
AYOS
BIVONA
C. DAI
A. DEFILIPPIS
GIANNONE
S. GUZZI
LAMBERTI
MARCHETTI
MARTINO
MENECHINO
D. REALI
SPARRY
J. SULLIVAN
VANCLEAF
VIGEANT
WISSEMAN

ABOUT THE AUTHOR

Tom Speedling, a New York native, received his Bachelor of Arts from St. Bonaventure University. After returning from Vietnam, he attained a Master's of Science Education from Richmond College. Mr. Speedling taught in New York city and state school systems for more than forty years. He has written two SAT prep books as well as numerous newspaper articles.

CPSIA information can be obtained
at www.ICGtesting.com
Printed in the USA
BVHW011404110722
641843BV00010B/412

9 781942 500810